Writeaerobics

40 Workshop Exercises to Improve Your Writing Teaching

Writeaerobics

40 Workshop Exercises to Improve Your Writing Teaching

by

Tommy Thomason

Christopher-Gordon Publishers, Inc.
Norwood, Massachusetts

Copyright Acknowledgments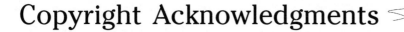

Christopher~Gordon Publishers, Inc.
Bridging Theory and Practice
1502 Providence Highway, Suite #12
Norwood, Massachusetts 02062
800-934-8322
781-762-5577

Printed in the United State of America
10 9 8 7 6 5 4 3 2 1   07 06 05 04 03

ISBN: 1-929024-61-4
Library of Congress Catalogue Number: 2003101607

For Debby,

a teacher's teacher,

and

Josh,

a musical artist who has taught me much

about teaching writing.

Contents

Preface

Confronting the Elephant

> The lyf so short, the craft so long to lerne.
>
> *Geoffrey Chaucer*

> There's an elephant in the room. It is large and squatting, so it is hard to get around it. Yet we squeeze by with, "How are you?" and "I'm fine," and a thousand other forms of trivial chatter. We talk about the weather. We talk about work. We talk about everything else, except the elephant in the room.
>
> *Anonymous*

Writing teachers have their own pedagogical pachyderm. When we get together, we talk about our students and about what we're doing in our writing classrooms. We talk about activities students seemed to enjoy. We talk about test scores on writing achievement tests and how we're preparing for those tests. We talk about books we're reading or writing seminars we've attended or plan to attend.

But the elephant is there.

Our "elephant" is the fact that so much we're doing just doesn't seem to be working. We're compulsively busy as writing teachers, but we still don't see the results we long for. And so many writing teachers still feel inadequate when it comes to what they should be doing to develop young writers.

What's wrong? For starters, most of us have not been trained to teach writing. There are only a handful of courses in schools of education designed to prepare young teachers to run a successful writing workshop. But what about the seminars on teaching writing and the multitude of books on the topic? Many are quite good, but they are destined to fail from the start.

Here's why. To teach writing well, you need three things:

First, you have to understand writing itself, as well as writing pedagogy. You need to understand descriptive writing, leads, dialogue, flashback techniques, revision, and the like. And you need to know how to run a writing workshop, how to help young writers choose their own topics, and how to conduct a shared writing or modeled writing session.

Second, you need to be a writer yourself. In fact, unless you write, you'll never really understand descriptive writing or dialogue techniques. You can teach about them, but they will just be words on a page. It'll be like a non-swimmer trying to teach swimming or a non-driver trying to teach driving or a non-gardener trying to teach gardening techniques.

Third, you need to know how to communicate your knowledge about writing effectively to your students. For example: As a writer, you have to deal constantly with writing leads for your pieces. Several times a week, you wrestle with the same thing your students face every time they begin a new piece in workshop. So you try to learn everything you can about leads and how writers craft engaging beginnings. You become a student of good leads and a collector of good leads. But now you have to take all that you have experienced yourself as a writer, and all that you know as a student of writing, and put together lessons that will help your young authors craft their own leads.

Workshops and books typically deal with one or occasionally even two of those three prerequisites for effective writing teaching. But all three have to be present for writing teaching to really work. Many teachers have tried to emphasize the third prerequisite—teaching effective writing lessons—without understanding writing themselves or experiencing life as a writer. And they have done a good job of presenting the content, but it hasn't worked because they are transferring information from their heads to those of their students instead of from their hearts and lives to the hearts and lives of would-be writers.

Thus this book. It isn't designed to be read all the way through. No more than you would read a recipe book all the way through. Sure, you might skim it to get a general idea of the contents, but a recipe book isn't meant for bedtime reading. It's designed to show you how to take a list of contents and, under the right conditions, turn them into something delicious. So you take it line by line. It tells you what ingredients you need, and you gather them. It says to combine butter and sugar, so you take those two ingredients and mix them together. When you think you have done that acceptably, you pick up the book and take the next step.

Writeaerobics is designed to be read—and worked through—in exactly the same way. Here's what you'll find in this book: 40 days of information (roughly two classroom months) about writing for you to think about, exercises to try in your own writing notebook, and activities to try with your own young writers. Some days you will read about truths about writing, other days about writing teaching. Then you will use that information in something you write in your notebook. Next, you will put together an activity or a craft lesson for your students on the same topic.

Can you finish in 40 days? Probably not. Don't take the workout 1, workout 2, workout 3 approach literally. If you want to spend longer in your writing notebook applying the skill discussed, don't hesitate to write on that topic for several days. The activities for your writing classroom might also take longer than one day. Often, you will come up with other ideas to extend the ideas given here. These 40 days might well extend to 60, or even 80. Don't worry about finishing it in a certain number days. After all, you are building teaching skills that will last a lifetime in the classroom.

This book was designed to help writing teachers acknowledge the elephant and to do something about it in the only way that makes sense—through better understanding of writing, through experiencing writing ourselves, and through translating our understanding and experience into classroom learning for our young writers.

How to Use the Workouts

The term aerobics was invented by exercise guru Dr. Kenneth Cooper in the late 1960s. Aerobics is an exercise program that increases your lung capacity (allowing them to take in more oxygen) and strengthens the heart (allowing it to pump oxygen more efficiently). And there are lots of other great benefits to aerobics, like lowering cholesterol and blood pressure, controlling weight, and controlling stress.

You enjoy the benefits of aerobics when you engage in aerobic exercises on a regular basis. It doesn't work overnight, but gradually you see the benefits.

Many people, when they realize they need to lose weight or get in shape, begin to study weight loss or buy books on exercise. Knowing the principles is good, but you can be an expert on fitness and be personally out of shape. Aerobics only works when you do it. And if you did it and didn't understand the physiology behind it, you'd still reap the benefits.

Writeaerobics applies that principle to writing. This book is based on the premise that writing ability—and teaching effectiveness in writing—isn't based on what you know, but what you do. Of course, there are things writing teachers need to know. But if that's as far as you go, you'll never be successful in your teaching.

Welcome to the *Writeaerobics* gym. Over the next few months, you'll tone up your writing muscles. You'll be reminded of some concepts you already know and learn new techniques. You'll apply those techniques first in your own writing—so buy yourself a writer's notebook. Then, you'll see how you can apply the concepts in your teaching. (Since this book is based on the value of keeping a writer's notebook, you may want to review the concept of a writer's notebook [as opposed to a journal] in appendix A.)

Each *Writeaerobic* workout includes the following:

✓ Quotes on writing to inspire you. Lots of the quotes you will find would make great posters for your classroom wall or effective discussion starters for craft lessons on writing.

✓ Short lessons on the writing craft or teaching writing.

✓ *Writeaerobic* exercises for your writer's notebook, so you can personally understand—and experience—the topic of that day's lesson.

✓ Ideas to build craft lessons for your writer's workshop.

Ready to get started? All you need is a few minutes a day to read the *Writeaerobics* lesson and from 10 to 15 minutes for your *Writeaerobics* workout.

Before long, your writing muscles will be feeling the burn.

Writeaerobics Workout #1

I Teach Writing, But I
Don't See Myself as a Writer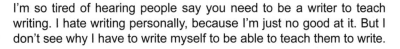

> I'm so tired of hearing people say you need to be a writer to teach writing. I hate writing personally, because I'm just no good at it. But I don't see why I have to write myself to be able to teach them to write.
>
> *Overheard in a faculty lounge*

> When we, as teachers, do not have good memories of writing to draw upon, we are apt to accept our students' resistance to writing as a given. When we assume that writing will always be a dreaded activity, we spend all our time pushing, luring, motivating, and bribing.
>
> *Lucy Calkins*

How do you explain chocolate to someone who has never tasted it? Or a rainbow to someone who has never seen one? Or personal freedom to someone in a repressive dictatorship who has never experienced the exhilaration of being able to speak and write freely? Or the value of being a writer to a teacher who has never written?

Many teachers have themselves never been in a classroom—from kindergarten through graduate school—where the teacher would come into class and say, "I was writing last night, and I just want to share a few paragraphs with you to see what you think."

Writing is not a set of academic principles or rules. It's a skill—much more similar to learning driving or cooking or karate than studying American history or science. We would never consider taking swimming classes from someone who could not swim or driving classes from someone who could not drive or even a wine appreciation class from someone who only talked about the differences in French and California Chardonnay from something he had read in a book on wines.

In fact, writing is perhaps the only skill taught largely by non-practitioners.

Why? Because we have been led to believe that we can teach a set of writing principles, guidelines, and rules, which, if followed, produce writers.

Does it work? Would you take non-swimmers and teach them a set of principles, guidelines, and rules of swimming and then throw them in the deep end?

To teach swimming you have to get wet—you teach swimming in the pool. And if writing instruction is to be effective, it has to be taught by people who themselves practice the craft.

Don't feel guilty if you're not writing yet. If you're not, you're just following the example of those who have taught you in writing classes over the years. But that's one of the purposes of this book. We'll guide you through, day by day, until you begin to see yourself as a writer.

In Your Writer's Notebook . . .

The first step toward writing regularly, and becoming a confident writer, is honestly confronting how you feel about writing. Today, write about your feelings on writing—whether you hate it or love it or something in between. Just be honest on paper. Try to identify why you feel like you do. If you don't like to write, chances are the reason has something to do with your experience in school.

In Your Classroom Writer's Workshop . . .

Let your writers brainstorm how people learn skills—playing football or ballet or martial arts, playing a musical instrument. You—and they—will be amazed to see the parallels between the way they learn, say, playing a guitar and the way they learn to write.

Writeaerobics Workout #2

Why Write?

> Why do kids play football? They can get hurt on any play, can't they? Yet they can't wait until Saturday comes around so they can play on the high school team, or the college team, and get smashed around. Writing is like that. You can get hurt, but you enjoy it.
>
> *Irwin Shaw*

> Why do I write? The truth, the unvarnished truth, is that I haven't a clue. The answer to that question lies hidden in the same box that holds the origin of human creativity, our imperative need as a species to communicate, and to be touched.
>
> *Gloria Naylor*

> To write is to write is to write is to write is to write is to write is to write is to write is to write.
>
> *Gertrude Stein*

Yesterday, we looked at writing from a completely utilitarian point of view—that writing teachers must themselves be writers to teach it effectively.

Today, let's get a little more spiritual. No one explained it better than writer/ writing teacher Julia Cameron (1998):

> Why should we write?
>
> We should write because it is human nature to write. Writing claims our world. It makes it directly and specifically our own. We should write because humans are spiritual beings and writing is a powerful form of prayer and meditation, connecting us both to our own insights and to a higher and deeper level of inner guidance as well.
>
> We should write because writing brings clarity and passion to the act of living. Writing is sensual, experiential, grounding. We should write because writing is good for the soul. We should write because writing

yields us a body of work, a felt path through the world we live in.

We should write, above all, because we are writers whether we call ourselves writers or not. The Right to Write is a birthright, a spiritual dowry that gives us the keys to the kingdom. Higher forces speak through the writing. Call them inspiration, the Muses, Angels, God, Hunches, Intuition, Guidance, or simply a good story—whatever you call them, they connect us to something larger than ourselves that allows us to live with greater vigor and optimism. . . .

I have a fantasy. It's the pearly gates. St. Peter has out his question-naire, he asks me the Big Question, "What did you do that we should let you in?"

"I convinced people they should write," I tell him. The great gates swing open. (pp. 230)

But if you're of a more practical bent, the question of why write? was also answered by writing coach Donald Murray (1987):

There are many side benefits to writing. Writing allows you to discover that you have a voice, a way of speaking that is individual and effective. It allows you to share with and even to influence others.

Writing can bring attention to you or to your ideas. It can add to your job skills, and it can improve your grades. Writing can give you power, for we live in a complicated technological society, and those people who can collect information, order it into significant meaning, and then communicate it to others will influence the course of events within the town or nation, school or university, company or corporation. Information is power.

If you have the ability to find specific, accurate information and fit it together in a meaningful pattern through language you will have the pleasure of making something that was not there before, or finding significance where others find confusion, or bringing order to chaos. If you can do this clearly and gracefully you will have readers, for people are hungry for specific information ordered into meaning. (pp. 3, 4)

Maybe you identify with Julia Cameron, or perhaps Don Murray best states the reasons most likely to motivate you to write. It really doesn't matter why you write. The recent Nike slogan probably states it best: "Just do it."

In Your Writer's Notebook . . .

In your writer's notebook, react to Julia Cameron's explanation of why we should write. Re-read it, then agree or disagree, or compare your experience with writing to the experience Ms. Cameron talks about.

In Your Classroom Writer's Workshop . . .

Looking at why writers write can be a valuable experience for young authors. You might begin by guiding them to think through why artists create—perhaps painters and sculptors and musicians. Then apply that to writing.

One of the most valuable things we can do for young writers is to help them see how professional writers and the world of writing/editing/illustrating/publishing works. There are a number of books that do just that. For a sampling of books that give young writers insights into the writing/illustrating/publishing process, see appendix D.

Writeaerobics Workout #3

How We Learn to Write

The only way to learn to write is to write. Robert Frost used to say that it is far more important that the student write than that the teacher correct what he or she writes.

Baird Whitlock

There is no one right way. Each of us finds a way that works for him. But there is a wrong way. The wrong way is to finish your writing day with no more words on paper than when you began. Writers write.

Robert Parker

If you wish to be a writer, write.

Epictetus

For years, we've been barking up the wrong trees, pedagogically speaking.

We're too concerned with new strategies and methods for teaching writing—not asking the basic question, "How do human beings learn to write?" Only after we answer that question can we design strategies and methods that help students learn.

Of course, there are different theories on the answer to that basic question. But there's one thing all writers agree on. All. Not most—all. It's this: You learn to write by writing. Not studying about writing. Not preparing to write. Not studying mechanics or conventions so your writing will be effective. All these things are good, but they work only for those who are already writing. You don't buy gourmet recipe books for someone who doesn't have a kitchen. First, you have to have a kitchen, and use it to prepare meals, and enjoy cooking, and want to improve and branch out and try new ideas. Then, you can begin to flight-test Julia Child's latest recipe.

We teach teens to drive by putting them behind the wheel of a car. Of course, we instruct and model, too, but everyone knows you don't learn to drive by listening to a parent explain the process or reading books or watching videos on driving. All those things have their place—in fact, they are necessary components of the process. But you learn to drive by actually driving.

Baird Whitlock (1986) tells the story of a freshman English teacher at San Jose State University who used an approach not typically found in college writing classes. He didn't "teach" writing. Instead, he simply told students to write for 50 minutes each class. Students had to keep writing, even if they only put down a string of *x*'s. A few did just that, but writing *x*'s gets boring after awhile, so they too began to write. They handed in their writing, but it was not handed back. The professor charted each student, including errors on mechanics. Amazingly, the writing began to get better on its own. Spelling improved first, then grammar, then punctuation. By the end of the semester this section was outperforming all traditionally taught sections.

The point is not that we stop teaching. It's that we realize that students must have time to write every day, across the curriculum, in authentic settings.

In Your Writer's Notebook . . .

Just write. Put your pen on the paper and freewrite. Write whatever comes to mind, paying no attention to train of thought, continuity, or even coherence. Set a time limit and don't stop until it expires.

In Your Classroom Writer's Workshop . . .

Try freewriting with your class. This strategy has traditionally been viewed as a prewriting exercise to get students ready to "really write." But freewriting *is* really writing.

Explain freewriting as a technique writers use to clear their mental cobwebs and stimulate their creativity. To freewrite, you just put pencil to paper and write. Your goal is not to write anything good, or anything creative, or even anything coherent. It is just to fill lines with words. You begin with an empty sheet. When you finish, it's full. Whether or not it even makes sense is absolutely irrelevant.

When you freewrite, you just keep the pencil moving. You never stop to think or plan or revise or correct. If you are describing the eraser you are looking at on the chalk tray and run out of anything else to say, you begin to write something like this: "I can't think of anything else to say about that eraser. I wish I could. I guess I have written everything anyone could possibly say about an eraser. They are pretty dull to write about. But I do wish I could have an eraser for my life and could go back and just erase some of the stuff I've done. Like being such a jerk last weekend with Susan. . . ."

Notice what happened. The writer ran out of anything to say and kept writing— about the fact that he had run out of anything to say. But in the last two sentences he did think of something, a metaphorical application of the eraser.

We believe that if we have a problem, it is beneficial to "talk it out." Just to keep on talking even though we don't know the answers. If we talk enough about what happened and how we reacted and how we feel, sometimes the answers just come to us as we talk. The same things happen with writing.

Explain to students that freewriting has 4 significant benefits: (a) It helps them find their writer's voice, because they are writing without constraints; (b) it serves as a compost pile of ideas for later pieces; (c) it helps them break free from their internal critics; and (d) it stimulates their creativity.

After you have explained freewriting, model it. If you have a video projector hooked up to a computer in your classroom, that's probably the best way to model. Just open a text file on your computer and let students see freewriting happen right there in front of them. Five minutes of this modeling is better than a half hour of explaining freewriting. If you don't have a video projector, slap a transparency down on your overhead projector and start freewriting.

For a more complete explanation of how freewriting works in a classroom setting, see Tommy Thomason and Carol York's (2002) *Absolutely Write! Teaching the Craft Elements of Writing.*

Writeaerobics Workout #4

Writing as a Discipline

Like running, the more you [write], the better you get at it. Some days you don't want to run and resist every step of the three miles, but you do it anyway. You practice whether you want to or not. Don't wait around for inspiration and a deep desire to run. It'll never happen, especially if you are out of shape and have been avoiding it. But if you run regularly, you train your mind to cut through or ignore your resistance. You just do it. And in the middle of the run, you love it. When you come to the end, you never want to stop. And you stop, hungry for the next time.

That's how writing is, too. Once you're deep into it, you wonder what took you so long to finally settle down at the desk. Through practice you actually get better. You learn to trust your deep self more and not give in to your voice that wants to avoid writing.

Natalie Goldberg

I write for a couple of hours every day, even if I only get a couple of sentences. I put in that time. You do that every day, and inspiration will come along. I don't allow myself not to keep trying.

Dave Barry

After losing more than 5,000 consecutive games as a pitcher, Charlie Brown walks off the mound in a famous *Peanuts* cartoon, looks up at heaven, and laments, "How can we lose when we're so sincere?"

They lost because they were a bad team. But sincerity is way overrated when it comes to writing, too. Lots of non-writers believe that you have to have some kind of sincere feeling, an overwhelming desire to write. That want-to, that sincere motivation, will lead you to write.

And so they wait for their muse to sing, or at least that sincere motivation to overtake them. It never does.

What's wrong? Go back and re-read Natalie Goldberg's comparison to running above. She says motivation doesn't produce running—instead, running produces motivation. And writing is the same. If you wait for motivation to write, you'll wait and wait. It probably won't come, and you'll never write.

Instead, forget the feeling. Forget the inspiration. Just write. People frequently say, "I want to write out of an overflowing desire to put pen to paper." They mistakenly believe that motivation produces writing. But what if they have it just backward, and it's writing that produces motivation?

In other words, we begin to write out of shear discipline. Maybe we don't want to. Maybe we don't really have anything to say. Maybe we don't enjoy it. We just make time, make a place, and sit down to get words on the paper. There's no motivation, no inspiration, no sincere desire to write, and perhaps no fulfillment in writing.

But as we write, it becomes a habit. It becomes a part of our day, and eventually of our lives. It becomes second nature to us. We eventually begin living like writers—thinking throughout the day as we observe people and events, "I could write about that." We develop fluency as writers. And eventually, we come to look forward to writing and we discover motivation. The motivation didn't cause us to write; instead, the writing led to our motivation.

In Your Writer's Notebook . . .

Write about a habit you have, either good or bad. How did you develop it?

In Your Classroom Writer's Workshop . . .

Take time in writer's workshop to talk about the concept of fluency and how writers develop it. Begin by defining the concept: Fluency is when you get so comfortable with anything that it becomes second-nature. Beginner pianists constantly look back and forth between their sheet music and their fingers. They look to see where a note is and what finger they should put there. More experienced pianists just play. Sometimes we note that they seem lost in the moment, perhaps even have their eyes closed. How can they do that? They are piano-fluent. They have played so much that they have a "feel" for where the notes are. Have students share things at which they have become fluent—perhaps dancing or sports or cooking or driving or sewing or playing video games.

Share with your young writers how sometimes writers don't feel like writing, but they do it anyway. Do teachers always feel like coming to school? Are they always excited about teaching? But even if you don't feel like teaching, you can still show up at school and still teach. And students can still learn on a day when you might have preferred to stay home in bed. Writers write, no matter how they feel. Writers "go to work" every day just like teachers and school crossing guards and police officers. That produces a comfort level with the act of writing that we call fluency. For more on developing fluency, see Tommy Thomason and Carol York's (2002) *Absolutely Write! Teaching the Craft Elements of Writing*.

Writeaerobics Workout #5

Whoever Said This Was Easy?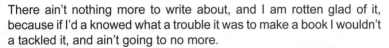

There ain't nothing more to write about, and I am rotten glad of it, because if I'd a knowed what a trouble it was to make a book I wouldn't a tackled it, and ain't going to no more.

Huckleberry Finn

Great practitioners in any field make it look easy, so bystanders murmur in awe about talent. What the bystander never sees is the agony of effort, study, and practice that made the final performance appear effortless—the fruits of a professional attitude.

Jack M. Bickham

There is a myth at large in the general population, easily quashable yet somehow allowed to persist, that writing comes smoothly, like gas from a pump, or at least unbidden, like tears. This is bull. No decent prose is ever dashed off, especially that which appears to be effortlessly dashing. Just as Buster Keaton and Douglas Fairbanks had to rehearse their leaps and pratfalls, so grace on the page has to be earned with infinite sweat.

Anthony Lane

Writing is so difficult that I often feel that writers, having had their hell on earth, will escape all punishment hereafter.

Jessamyn West

Huck Finn's idea above has been echoed by writers over the years. Many writers have talked about just how difficult the craft is, how they agonize over what they write. Many writers tell young people asking about writing not to become a writer unless they have a really strong inner compulsion—almost an obsession—to do it. Otherwise, the veteran writers say, they'll never make it. It's too hard unless you're *driven* to write.

And then you hear others talking about writing, and they say anyone can learn to write. True, there is a talent for writing that some have, and this talent makes it much easier for them. But anyone can learn to produce readable, even excellent, prose. Writing, like cooking or swimming or woodworking or driving, is a craft that can be learned.

Who's right? The unfortunate answer, of course, is both. If you have studied under writing teachers who were themselves writers, this will seem obvious. If your writing teachers were just teachers of writing, not teachers who wrote, this will probably come off as a paradox to you.

The reconciliation of these two disparate ideas is at the heart of the writing process itself. Talented writers seem to be able to produce good writing naturally, sometimes with little instruction. They are like the musicians who sit down at the piano at an early age, with little or no teaching, and begin to play beautiful music. But most musicians, and most writers, are not prodigies. They had to learn to play or to write from a teacher.

The better the musician, the more effortless the music often seems. You listen as the fingers of the pianist trip across the keys, drawing you into his or her world of artistry. What you don't see is the hours upon hours of practice, day after day, it took to produce what seems to be talent or effortless artistry on the stage.

Anyone can learn to write, but writing well is hard work. Writers sometimes spend hours working on a word or phrase to get it just right. . . . hours on a phrase you will read in just a few seconds. Ernest Hemingway once told an interviewer that he rewrote the last page of *Farewell to Arms* 39 times before he was satisfied with it. The interviewer asked the great author what had him stumped.

"Getting the words right," Hemingway replied.

Novelist Larry L. King said he works on each sentence until he is satisfied with it.

"I may rewrite one sentence 19 times, and the next sentence eight times, and the next sentence three times," King said. "When I'm lucky, one sentence once."

So while writers enjoy writing, they see it as hard work. When teachers are themselves writers, they understand that, and pass that perspective along to their young authors.

In Your Writer's Notebook . . .

Write about how you have learned to write, and how you have developed the abilities you have. Assess any role you think talent played versus the role of craft.

In Your Classroom Writer's Workshop . . .

Work on a craft lesson on writing as talent versus writing as a craft. Don't just assume that your young writers understand these distinctions. Talk about talent in music and athletics, and what it means when someone is naturally talented. Then talk about the things people don't know how to do but learn under the guidance of an experienced practitioner—like cooking or driving or swimming or judo or painting or ballet. With your class, discuss how people learn to write, as opposed to how they learn other skills. You might want to pick a skill they are familiar with (like swimming) and ask them how people learn to swim. You should be able to draw many parallels between the way people learn to swim and the way they learn to write.

Writeaerobics Workout #6

The Critic Inside Your Head

If we wait until the fear of writing goes away, we will never write.

Susan Shaughnessy

It is the fear of "What will people think?" that the inner critic . . . uses to paralyze us. That and "But it isn't perfect. You must make it perfect. And if you can't make it perfect, don't bother writing at all." The only way out of this trap is to concentrate on your writing: selecting words, stringing phrases together, forming sentences, rewriting, and so on. There are enough paid critics, marketing strategists, and publicists to evaluate your work. And they will. You don't have to do it for them.

Cathleen Rountree

If you lived in ancient Greece, one of the deities you would have had to appease was Momus, the god of criticism and faultfinding. And while most Greek gods are relegated to textbooks on ancient history, Momus still lives in the soul of writers—and anyone who ever even tried to write.[1]

Momus is your internal editor, your critic. He's the nagging voice inside your head when you write. If you're a perfectionist, you probably even honor Momus. After all, he's the one who won't let you settle for second best, the one who demands you always produce your best work, the one who won't let you use a word you can't spell or a grammatical construction you're unsure of. For many, he is the god of exacting standards.

But it is this internal critical voice that keeps us from writing. Writers believe one set of simple, probably even simplistic, truths: Writing is good; not writing is bad. Anything that facilitates writing is good; anything that stops you from writing is bad—even if what is stopping you is the voice encouraging you not to write until you can check the spelling of a word or get a better idea or make an outline before you proceed. So veteran writers disregard the voice that tells them to postpone writing or tells them that their writing doesn't measure up.

Rebecca Rule and Susan Wheeler (1993) note that this internal critic is destructive to writers when they write but perhaps useful when they turn to editing and revision:

> Most writers have nagging critics whose voices can sometimes get so loud and destructive that the writers can't write. Here are some of the things inner critics like to say: This stinks! Who cares? Your grammar is terrible. You always were a bore and this is boring too. You're so damned slow at writing, and this is so hard to do, you might as well clean out the garage and write later. Face it, you lack talent and brains. Why don't you quit now and become an accountant?
>
> Each of us must control his own critic. Tell your critic to go away for now. Later, you will ask her back when she can help you with spelling and grammar, and check to see if you've developed your scenes enough, or if you need to delve more deeply into your main character. It's important to assure the critic that she will be of use later. That way, she'll go away more readily when she isn't needed.
>
> Most internal critics fear failure. They are crippled by this fear. They would never have the courage to dive into stories without knowing what would happen next. (p. 49)

In Your Writer's Notebook . . .

Write about your internal critic. How strong is he/she? Do you hear the critic's voice when you write? Do you fear making mistakes or fear failing to meet the standards you have set for your writing? And be honest now: Do you fear modeling writing in front of your students? Write about your critic's tactics when you write. You might even start a list in the back of your writer's notebook of the things your critic will typically put into your mind when you write. List and number them all and think about what your response should be. As new things come up when you write, add them to the list. Your critic might be creative, but she's not that creative. Pretty soon, as you write, something will come into your mind, perhaps "This is awful, and you call yourself a writer!" And you'll say, "Well, old No. 37, huh? Come on, Momus, we dealt with that stupid argument months ago. You'll have to do better than that!" And you'll keep on writing.

In Your Classroom Writer's Workshop . . .

Introduce the idea of the critic to your students. Perhaps you'd like to call him Momus. Have your students draw Momus and talk about how he discourages them when they write. Once they have personified the critic and identified his tactics, you'll hear them addressing Momus under their breath as they write.

Endnote

[1] According to Greek myth, the first man was made by Jupiter, the first bull by Neptune, and the first house by Minerva. When they finished their labors, they began to argue over whose work was more perfect. They agreed to appoint Momus as the judge and to abide by his decision. Momus, however, was envious of their work and criticized each one as being inadequate in some way. Jupiter, indignant over such inveterate faultfinding, drove him from his office as judge and expelled him from Olympus. The point here, obviously, is that writers must take their cue from Jupiter and expel Momus from their writing lives.

Writeaerobics Workout #7

Writing Garbage: Why You Should Lower Your Standards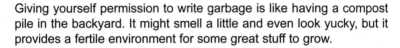

> Giving yourself permission to write garbage is like having a compost pile in the backyard. It might smell a little and even look yucky, but it provides a fertile environment for some great stuff to grow.
>
> *Henriette Anne Klauser*

One of Momus' best-sounding lies is that you should always do your best work when you write. Here's the way it sounds: Always do your best work. It's better not to write at all than to do poor work or write about something you don't care about, or write when you don't want to write and you're sure your work won't reflect the quality you know you can produce. It's better to wait until you have a good idea, your mind is clear, and you're really ready to write.

And if you believe that, we can guarantee one thing: You'll never become a writer. Momus, you see, is a liar. He says he wants you to produce quality. What he knows is that if you wait for quality, you'll put off writing and you'll probably never write.

Momus' great invention to facilitate his wishes is the concept of the "writer's block." What a wonderful idea—you can't write because you are not inspired, no ideas are coming, and you are certain to produce garbage if you try.

All professional writers know that writer's block doesn't exist. To be sure, there are many days when professional writers do not want to write. When they have no ideas. When they feel lousy or physically sick or just sick of writing. Days when they have nothing to write about and nothing to say. What do pros do on those days?

They write, of course.

What do you do as a teacher when you wake up and feel yucky or headachy or just don't want to go to work that day? Maybe you wake up and the last thing you want to be around that day is children! What do you do? Call in with "teacher's block"? No, you go to work anyway. You have discovered that you can teach, and students can learn, even when you'd rather be anywhere else doing anything else other than teaching.

The best antidote to writer's block is to write. You begin by lowering your standards. If you can't write well, write poorly. If you have nothing to say, then write about nothing—or write about the fact that your life is so boring you have nothing to say. Just write, and don't let Momus judge the quality.

Some days, you will write garbage. But occasionally, what starts out as garbage will turn into something good. And occasionally, you will look at the garbage you wrote yesterday and it will give you an idea for something you'd really like to write. Or today's rewrite of yesterday's garbage turns out to be your best piece in a month.

In Your Writer's Notebook . . .

Today, write about writer's block and how writers should deal with it. Think specifically of your students. What advice would you give them when they have nothing to write about? How does today's workout apply to a fourth grader (or whatever grade you teach)?

In Your Classroom Writer's Workshop . . .

Once you've thought through and written about today's workout in your writer's notebook, turn it into a craft lesson for your writer's workshop.

Writeaerobics Workout #8

Choosing Topics:
What Do I Write About?

> I wrote about schools because half of the young people go to schools.
> And I wrote about cars. Half of the people have cars. And mostly all
> the people, if they're not, they'll soon be in love. . . . So wrote about all
> three and I think it hit a pretty good group of the people.
>
> *Chuck Berry*

"I have nothing to write about. Nothing ever happens in my life."

It's the non-writer's mantra. Actually, it's just a lame excuse not to write. But it comes from a more basic problem among non-writers: They have mystified writing.

"Mystified" means to see something as mysterious and unattainable. To see writing—or any other skill—as something others can do, but not us.

Imagine yourself on playground duty. Three boys come running up to you to tell you they're going to play dodgeball. They say that when they play, they have to line up to take their turn. Sometime they wait in line for several minutes. They plead with you: "Please, can you write down something for us to talk about while we're in line? So we don't have to just stand there and look at each other and be bored?"

You know that would never happen. Kids always have lots to talk about—even when we want them to be quiet and listen. And what do they talk about? Movies, TV shows, music, pets, parents, friends, sports, gossip, school, and, of course, their teacher. They never lack topics of conversation. But those same kids will stare at a piece of paper during writing workshop and moan, "I have nothing to write about." Why? Because they have mystified writing. They see talking and writing differently. They talk about what interests them. What they love. What they hate. What they do and watch and listen to. What they think. What's happening. Writers know this is also what we write about. Writers know that the things that interest them and fill their thoughts are also their writing topics.

Writing teacher Joel Saltzman (1993) tells this story about one of his students:

> Mary Cahill, a suburban housewife with two teenagers, once joked
> that if she were to write a novel, "I would have to write about what I
> know, and I would have to call it *Carpool*." Accepting the challenge,
> she sat down and wrote a novel: *Carpool: A Novel of Suburban*

Frustration. Nine rejections and one rewrite later, she sold her manuscript to Random House. *Carpool* became a Literary Guild main selec-
tion and Viacom bought the right to turn it into a television movie. (p.
55)

In Your Writer's Notebook . . .

Make a list of topics you could write about in the future. Use the following list as
topic headings and write down as many specific topics as you can. Keep the list in
your writer's notebook. When you talk with your students about topic choice, share
some of the topics in your writer's notebook. Here are your topic headings: memories of childhood involving my parents, memories of my childhood involving school
(keep going here with memories of your childhood involving pets, friends, athletics,
church, fears, vacations, you name it).

In Your Classroom Writer's Workshop . . .

One of your primary functions as a writing teacher is to show students how to think
like writers. And that involves taking them off writer's welfare—the idea that students need teachers to dole out topics and prompts every day because they have
nothing to write about.

Take the topics below and put them into a graphic organizer that students can fill
out. Tell them it isn't necessary to write something in every space, just the ones
where something springs immediately to mind. After they have filled in their topics,
let a few share what they wrote down. This primes the writing pump and gives
others ideas about similar topics.

Have your students put their graphic organizers into their writing folders as a
"rainy day writing contingency" for when they need a topic. And be sure to remind
them frequently that whenever they come up with a good writing topic, to add it to
their list. The more they write, and the more literature and craft lessons you share,
the longer their lists will become. And they'll never run out of something to write
about.

Here are some topics to get you started (you'll come up with many more yourself): music I like; things I know a lot about; things I am good at; games I like to
play; someone who is really important to me, and why; something I care about;
places I like to go; things that make me happy; things that make me sad; things that
make me angry; something I want to do some day. Adapt the list according to your
grade level. Don't be afraid to spend class time letting students share what is on their
lists. Ask them questions about what they share—the kinds of questions they would
need to answer if they wrote about that topic.

Writing Is for
Reading—Out Loud

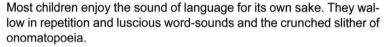

> Most children enjoy the sound of language for its own sake. They wallow in repetition and luscious word-sounds and the crunched slither of onomatopoeia.
>
> *Ursula K. LeGuin*

Writing is talk on paper.

And for centuries before humans wrote, they told stories and passed information along orally. Even when they began to write, the flavor of orality remained.

Imagine an ancient Greek storyteller enthralling his Athenian listeners as he began the story of Homer's *Odyssey*. Or perhaps you have been comforted to hear the words of the psalmist David: "The Lord is my shepherd, I shall not want." Right now, experience the power of language by reading the opening stanza of John Masefield's *Sea Fever* out loud:

> *I must go down to the seas again, to the lonely sea and sky,*
>
> *All I ask is a tall ship and a star to steer her by,*
>
> *And wheel's kick and the wind's song and white sail's shaking,*
>
> *And a gray mist on the sea's face and a gray dawn breaking.*

Marshall McLuhan (1962) in *The Gutenberg Galaxy* shows us how the medium (print) influences the content of the medium (stories and information). In other words, the writing changes if it is meant to be read silently as opposed to being read out loud.

But still, some writing just begs to be read orally (like Edgar Allen Poe's *The Raven* or *The Bells*, Lewis Carroll's *Jabberwocky*, or Bill Martin Jr. and John Archambault's picture book *Listen to the Rain*).

Many writers give their pieces the "read-aloud test." They read everything aloud to check the flow, the pacing, the juxtaposition of subjects and verbs or nouns and modifiers. Sentences that are hard to read aloud—though they may be "correct" in conventions—are frequently also hard to read silently.

Most of us read silently—because we realize we'd look a little odd reading out loud on an airplane or waiting in the dentist's office or while soaking up the sun at the beach. But sometimes, when you're by yourself and you're struck with the beauty of a piece of prose or poetry, try reading it out loud. . . . just to experience the power of the language.

In Your Writer's Notebook . . .

Write a paragraph designed for reading aloud. Use alliteration, repetition, rhythm, dialect—any sound effect you can think of. If you're stuck for an idea, read Bill Martin Jr. and John Archembault's (1988) *Listen to the Rain*, and try the same idea as Listen to the Wind or Listen to the Sounds of Summer or Listen to the Sounds of a Classroom.

In Your Classroom Writer's Workshop . . .

Students enjoy reading their words out loud. They also like for their teachers to read their words to the whole class. Occasionally, when you discover a piece—or just a paragraph—that you can celebrate in oral reading, ask the student if you can read it to the class during share time.

Then say something like this: "Today, Anne Marie shared something with me in our conference that just needs to be read out loud. She has given me permission to share it with the class. Now listen to this. . . ." Then, given an oral performance of Anne Marie's piece that holds back nothing. Put every bit of your acting ability and oral eloquence into reading this piece. If you have neither acting ability nor oral eloquence, fake it . . . but do it with passion and gusto.

And watch the face of the young writer whose work you are sharing. You are giving that author a memory-gift a writer of any age would treasure.

Writeaerobics Workout #10

Literary Tone Deafness:
Developing An Ear for Writing

> Whenever we read something and like it, we inevitably store it away in our model-chamber. And it goes with a myriad of its fellows to the building, brick by brick, of the eventual edifice which we call our style.
>
> *Mark Twain*

> Usually we write with our ears leading the way.
>
> *Baird Whitlock*

> I think writing is imitative. When I sit down to write, I know that I hear in my head the rhythms of writers I have read and admired. Sometimes, I can even remember which writer's rhythms I am hearing. I think all the good writers hear the music of good writing they've read.
>
> *Charles Kuralt*

One secret to effective writing is too good to be true, to simple to seem credible: Reading well-written prose and poetry will make you a better writer.

Sure, it doesn't work overnight or in isolation from other writing improvement strategies. And there seems to be only one group of people who think it's really important: good writers.

Like these:

> Writing is a difficult trade which must be learned slowly by reading great authors, by trying at the outset to imitate them.
>
> *Andre Maurois*

> When I read Ray Bradbury as a kid, I wrote like Ray Bradbury—everything green and wondrous and seen through a lens smeared with the grease of nostalgia. When I read James M. Cain, everything I wrote

came out clipped and stripped and hardboiled. When I read Lovecraft, my prose became luxurious and Byzantine. I wrote stories in my teenage years where all these styles merged, creating a hilarious stew. This sort of stylistic blending is a necessary part of developing one's own style. . . . You have to read widely, constantly refining (and redefining) your own work as you do so. . . . If you don't have time to read, you don't have the time (or the tools) to write. Simple as that.

Stephen King

Schools have little time for this strategy that writers consider so important, because the non-writers in charge of curriculum don't see how just reading—or even listening to a book being read—can make you a better writer.

Instead, they reason, filling out grammar worksheets, writing to a teacher-made prompt, or outlining a plot should be much more effective in helping young writers. They can read on their own time, and being read to is something for young primaries.

So these non-writing simpletons put together curriculum like a 6-year-old makes a castle out of Legos—everything fits nicely but it only vaguely resembles a "real" castle.

The result: Many children are growing up with literary tone-deafness. They don't have experience listening to beautiful language, or the rich storehouse of vocabulary and feel for language and story that are so important for anyone who wants to learn to write.

So what are you doing to improve yourself as a writer? You're writing. And you're reading this book, and others like it on writing and writing teaching. But don't forget: Every time you read a well-written book you are building your inner storehouse of language and genre and writing technique.

In Your Writer's Notebook . . .

Read the following paragraph from Dickens' (1859) *A Tale of Two Cities*. In your writer's notebook, tell why you think this is one of the most often-quoted passages ever penned in English.

It was the best of times, it was the worst of times, it was the age of wisdom, it was the age of foolishness, it was the epoch of disbelief, it was the epoch of incredulity, it was the season of Light, it was the season of Darkness, it was the spring of Hope, it was the winter of despair, we had everything before us, we had nothing before us, we were all going direct to Heaven, we were all going direct the other way—in short, the period was so far like the present period, that some of its noisiest authorities insisted on its being received, for good or for evil, in the superlative degree of comparison only. (p. 1)

In Your Classroom Writer's Workshop . . .

Talk about the importance of beautiful music to the listener, beautiful art to the viewer, and beautiful language to the reader. Let students try to recall examples from books they have read or books you have read aloud in class. Be sure to have some of those books—especially poetry collections—available on a nearby table. Students probably can't quote a passage that struck them, but many can pick up the book and turn to the words they especially enjoyed. Then, let students look through their writer's notebooks and come up with one sentence or even one phrase of their own which they consider to be "beautiful language."

Writeaerobics Workout #11

A Feel for the Language

Each of us has a linguistic storehouse into which we deposit patterns for stories and poems and sentences and words. These patterns enter the memory through the ear and remain available, ready to be cued into action, throughout the whole of a lifetime, providing advance information that is valuable for reading, writing, speaking, listening, and thinking.

Bill Martin Jr.

Before electronic media came to dominate our attention and our time, people had more time for reading. Reading aloud was more common in homes and more common in the classroom. George Higgins (1990) in his book *On Writing* explains a potential effect on young writers:

The majority of American children entering the world since the fifties ended seem not to possess what for want of a better term may be called a feel for the language. When some of those former children, now independent adults, find their way into journalism and creative writing, they commonly display utter ignorance of the cadence and rhythm of the American language, so that all the richness that it delivers off the tongue—their tongues as much as anyone else's—vanishes in their translation of it to the written word. The sensory aspect of the language disappears in their transcriptions of it *because their instruction in it never called that aspect of it to their attention.* [Emphasis added.]

Fortunately, this condition is curable, at any stage in life. All that is necessary is for you to do for yourself what was not done for you by your parents or other family members when you were young, either because you were watching television and could not be disturbed, or because they were watching television and did not wish to be: read good prose aloud. (pp. 8, 9)

Higgins is a novelist, not a teacher. But he recognizes what most writers know: that reading aloud is a crucial part of creating writers.

For years now, non-writers have dominated writing instruction. Work-sheets and prompt-driven writing assignments and preparation for standardized testing have crowded out classroom writing time. Reading aloud was considered a waste of valuable instructional time.

And no one—except writers and teachers—understood the eventual disastrous results of losing time just to read great writing aloud.

In Your Writer's Notebook . . .

A writer's notebook is really a writer's workshop—a place to experiment with writing (see appendix A). So some days we experiment in ways that do not even involve writing. Today is one of those days.

You might want to try Higgins' own prescription for developing a feel for language. He suggests shutting yourself in a room for 20 minutes a day and reading aloud from E. B. White's (1952) *Charlotte's Web* or another well-written book, until you begin to "feel" how writers use language.

Don't just dismiss Higgins' idea as impractical. Did you read the excerpt from Dickens' *A Tale of Two Cities* in yesterday's workout? Try reading it again, maybe for several days. Or pick a poem you really like. And when you find a paragraph in a book you really enjoy, take a few extra minutes to re-read it—aloud.

In Your Classroom Writer's Workshop . . .

Read a well-written excerpt to your class. Then tell students you will read it again, but you want them to listen like writers. When you finish, let them list the words, phrases, verbs, literary devices, and so forth, that make the piece effective. Or just let them recall phrases they really liked. Write those on the board and let them sink in for your young writers.

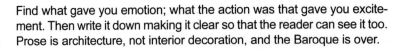

Description: Forget the Thesaurus and Observe

Find what gave you emotion; what the action was that gave you excitement. Then write it down making it clear so that the reader can see it too. Prose is architecture, not interior decoration, and the Baroque is over.

Ernest Hemingway

I don't tell; I don't explain. I show; I let my characters talk for me.

Tolstoy

The thesaurus is typically a tool for non-writers.

Here's how it works: The non-writer attempting to write feels her prose is mundane, so she opens the thesaurus looking for a big, impressive word to substitute for a more common word. And though *colorful* might be overused, *polychromatic* just substitutes a longer word—one fewer people can recognize. The prose becomes dense and hard to read.

The alternative? Stop looking at the thesaurus and start looking at what you are trying to describe. Use sensory details—colors, shapes, smells, textures—that readers will be able to picture. This good advice comes from author Rebecca McClanahan (1999):

> Concrete nouns will anchor your description. Use only those adjectives that call forth the qualities of the object; avoid adjectives that label or explain. Words like lovely, old, wonderful, noteworthy, or remarkable are explanatory labels; they do not suggest sense impressions. Adjectives like bug-eyed, curly, bumpy, frayed, or moss-covered, on the other hand, are descriptive. (p. 17)

When we go to a thesaurus, we're looking for someone else's word. Instead, we need to picture what we are trying to describe. How does it look? Describe it to a blind person. Are there associated sounds or smells?

Prose we remember is written by authors who paint word pictures on paper. The movie *Harry Potter and the Sorcerer's Stone* broke box-office records and held audiences enthralled. But for years before director Chris Columbus delighted viewing audiences, J. K. Rowling had amassed a following of literally millions of children and adults with the Harry Potter series. When Columbus made the movie, he had professional actors and lavish sets and state-of-the-art special effects. But Rowling had already built a huge army of fans. . . . using the 26 letters of the English alphabet and spaces. Nothing else. Harry Potter fans who went to the movie were going to see if Columbus' pictures were faithful to the pictures already in their heads.

Who put those pictures there? J. K. Rowling did, using letters and spaces . . . and a commitment to painting word pictures for her readers.

In Your Writer's Notebook . . .

Go to the store and buy a piece of fruit. Make it something you're not accustomed to eating or haven't eaten in a long time—maybe a kiwi or a green apple. First, just set the fruit on the table and look at it; then describe its shape and color and size. Next, cut the fruit. Touch it, press it, poke it, and write about the texture and feel. Then, write about the smell. Taste it and write about the taste. When you finish, you'll be amazed at how much you can write about a piece of fruit. . . . and how you can make the piece of fruit real to a reader.

In Your Classroom Writer's Workshop . . .

Take your "fruit piece" to class and read it, using *X* or some made-up word to substitute for the name of the fruit. Let your students guess what it is. They'll want to try it, too. You can use fruit or even a piece of chocolate. If you use chocolate, you might want to read them Gloria Houston's (1992) description of eating a Hershey bar in *But No Candy*.

Show, Don't Tell:
Bringing Writing to Life

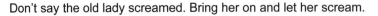

Don't say the old lady screamed. Bring her on and let her scream.

Mark Twain

Description begins with visualization of what you want the reader to experience. It ends with your translating what you want to see in your mind into words on a page.

Stephen King

Inexperienced writers tell; professionals show.

New writers tell you someone is beautiful or courageous or naive or sneaky. More experienced writers show you those qualities through things their characters say or do.

Let's say you're writing about your fifth-grade teacher. You could say: Mrs. Smith was loving and caring and I'll never forget her. Or you could show those qualities instead of telling your reader about them:

> I'll never forget that warm April afternoon when our class came in from recess. There were tears in my eyes, but I didn't think Mrs. Smith noticed. I heard her tell the class to get our arithmetic books and begin working on the problems on page 237. As I pulled my book from underneath my desk, Mrs. Smith walked up to my desk and knelt beside me, her lips only inches from my ear. "Jayne, what's wrong?" she asked gently. "Nothing," I lied. "I'm OK." Then she put her hand gently on my arm and said, softly and more slowly, but insistently, "Jayne . . . what's . . . wrong?" The whole story came rolling out, amidst my tears, how my best friend Sara had told me on the playground that she didn't want to be my friend any more and how I thought I would never be happy again. As other children worked on long division, Mrs. Smith quietly took me to her desk, where we talked about what had happened, and I re-discovered hope.

Those sentences never say Mrs. Smith was a concerned or caring or loving teacher. Instead, they tell the story, and the reader can discover it for herself.

Robert Newton Peck (1980) explained it this way in his *Secrets of Successful Fiction:*

> Readers want a picture—something to see, not just a paragraph to read. A picture made out of words. That's what makes a pro out of an amateur. An amateur tells a story. A pro shows a story, creates a picture to look at instead of just words to read. A good author writes with a camera, not with a pen.
>
> The amateur writes: "Bill was nervous."
>
> The pro writes: "Bill sits in a dentist's waiting room, peeling the skin at the edge of his thumb, until the raw, red flesh began to show. Biting the torn cuticle, he ripped it away, and sucked at the warm sweetness of his own blood." (p. 4)

This kind of writing puts pictures in the mind of the reader—because the prose or poetry is full of images and sensory detail.

In Your Writer's Notebook . . .

Write these three sentences in your writer's notebook:

> Doris was upset.
>
> Doris was naive.
>
> Doris was courageous.

Each of those sentences tells the reader something about Doris. Today, in your notebook, show instead. When Doris was upset, for instance, what did she say? What did she do? How did she look? Write several sentences about Doris that never mention the word "upset." But the reader should be able to read those sentences and come away saying, "Gosh, Doris was upset, wasn't she?"

In Your Classroom Writer's Workshop . . .

After you have tried the writer's notebook exercise yourself, try it on your students. Some teachers like to do this as a warm-up exercise for writer's workshop. Start with a list of character qualities: ambitious, anxious, brave, caring, dependable, fearful, friendly, happy, lazy, nervous, patient, petty, playful, reliable, responsible, sarcastic, shy, vain. You can add more as time goes on. Take one character and use that same character in a three-word sentence every day: Doris was ambitious, Doris was anxious, Doris was brave, and so forth. On Monday, put up a sentence like "Doris was jealous." Ask your young authors to imagine Doris and her jealousy. Have them actually picture her. Then say something like this: "Can you tell when someone is jealous? Have you ever seen someone and thought, 'They are really jealous!' Of course you have. But did that person tell you, 'I'm jealous'? Of course not. They said something or did something that you saw, and then you knew they were jealous. When writers write, they don't just tell you someone was jealous. They do it like real life—they show you someone saying something or doing something, and you come to the conclusion that they are a jealous person. So let's take Doris here. Imagine Doris is someone you know. What might you see her doing or hear her saying that would make you say she's jealous? Write that down in no more than three sentences. You cannot use the word jealous or envious. But when I read your sentence, I should definitely know Doris is jealous. Young writers will enjoy this show, don't tell exercise. You might want to start out using this as a 10-minute craft lesson for several days. Then keep doing it, but do it as a 5-minute warm-up. After you've done it for several weeks, you will begin to see more and more descriptive writing in your students' pieces.

Writeaerobics Workout #14

Everyone Has a Story

This is what a story is not: It is not an essay, not an exploration of an idea, although ideas will be present. If you find yourself thinking, Oh, I have this great idea about two characters who meet and then they do this or that which will illustrate their existential crises, beware. You're writing to prove a theory rather than writing to discover insights about a character. . . . A story bred of an idea or written to prove a point is doomed.

Rebecca Rule and Susan Wheeler

If you have a skeleton in your closet, take it out and dance with it.

Susan Shaughnessy

You might not see yourself as a storyteller, but you probably are. You tell stories orally every day, stories that probably need to be written in your writer's notebook. Some could be told on paper just as you tell them to your colleagues in the teachers' lounge. Others can be adapted through changing events or adding characters or modifying setting.

Think about the stories you tell to your friends, family, and colleagues. You tell stories about what happens in your class, about your crazy relatives, about the mean-spirited professor in your evening graduate class, about getting stopped by a motor-cycle police officer, about the man who flirted with you in the supermarket.

Professional writers draw heavily on their own experience. But they use their experiences to inspire their stories, to kick off the creative process. Beginning with their realities, they add characters, embellish the elements of suspense, add new conflicts, change the setting, and sometimes provide a completely different ending. They aren't concerned that they haven't been true to their experience; they are more interested in being true to their calling as a storyteller. (If you're honest, you'll prob-ably admit that you've done the same thing—perhaps added a little dialogue to dem-onstrate how you gave the motorcycle officer a piece of your mind when all you really said was "Thank you, officer." All storytellers tweak their realities in the inter-est of improving the plot.)

It's important here to draw the distinction between stories and narratives: Though many people use the term interchangeably, they're not the same thing. A narrative is a chronological accounting of events. If you tell what happened to you since you woke up today, it's probably just a narrative. You are recounting what happened, as it happened. And it's probably fairly uninteresting. But let's say, on your way to work, another driver cuts you off on the freeway and you hit a guardrail. The narrative has turned into a story—there's a problem to deal with. Perhaps the other driver stops and blames you for the accident and now you have tension and conflict.

That conflict, and how you handle it, reveals something about you as the main character. And if it's good enough to tell to your friends, it's good enough to write about and perhaps to embellish to make it even more interesting to the reader.

Think back to stories you read in class or novels you have enjoyed. Pay attention to how the writer focuses on a character in trouble. Look at where the conflict is introduced—at the beginning, or do you get to know the characters first? When you read a novel, don't just read like a reader; read like a writer. Enjoy the novel, but look at what information the writer shares about the characters so you will care about them. Notice the same things in your novel that you are probably teaching in language arts: rising action, crisis point (where the drama comes to a head), falling action, and resolution. What do you learn that you can use in writing your own stories?

In Your Writer's Notebook . . .

Try to remember two or three stories you have told recently. Tell those stories on paper, trying to write them just like you told them orally. Then, make a little chart about the stories, identifying the conflict, the characters, the rising action, the crisis point, the falling action, and the resolution. Could your stories be changed to make them even better? They wouldn't be true to your reality that way, but they might make much better reading.

In Your Classroom Writer's Workshop . . .

Share some of your writer's notebook work on stories with your class. Show them how you can take an oral story and write about it.

This is actually a high-level skill, one that's very difficult for young writers—taking a real-life story and adapting it to print. Here's how you can use your own stories to teach your writers about story construction:

1. Orally tell one of the stories you wrote in your writer's notebook. Feel free to add information that isn't in the written version.

2. Then, let your class ask you questions about what happened—information that they are interested in that wasn't in your oral telling.

3. Next, share the written version of that story from your writer's notebook. Make copies or a transparency for your students so they can follow along as you read.

4. Let your students identify various story elements in your written version (problem, resolution, rising and falling action, etc.) as appropriate to their grade level. You might even want to let them do a story map on your written piece.

5. Ask if any of the elements in your oral version, or information generated in your answers to any of the questions your students asked, should be added to the story. If they suggest revisions that most of the class agrees on, you are now set up for the next day's craft lesson on revision, as you talk about why writers make changes and how they go about incorporating those changes into the text.

Writeaerobics Workout #15

The Six Traits
of Effective Writing

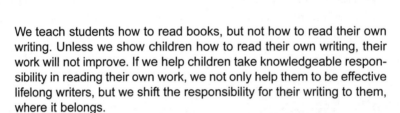

> We teach students how to read books, but not how to read their own writing. Unless we show children how to read their own writing, their work will not improve. If we help children take knowledgeable responsibility in reading their own work, we not only help them to be effective lifelong writers, but we shift the responsibility for their writing to them, where it belongs.
>
> *Donald Graves*

> If . . . children can't talk easily about texts, they will have a hard time being critical readers of their own or anyone else's writing.
>
> *Lucy Calkins*

Think back to when you were in school—from first grade through graduate school—and your teachers assessed your writing. You wrote, you turned in the piece, and it came back with a grade, with editing marks (probably in red), and perhaps with notes in the margin. For most of us, this represents our own personal exposure to writing assessment. All too frequently, the grade reflected our grammar and spelling and punctuation and usage (to or too, affect or effect, their or there). Perhaps it also reflected the extent to which we followed directions—whether we turned in an outline, did the bibliography correctly, and the like. But what about the composition, the writing itself? Was it assessed? And if so, how?

Perhaps you enjoy reading movie reviews to help you decide which movie you'll go to. What you're reading is a movie assessment. A good reviewer will assess the acting, the directing, the script, the music, and the cinematography. If the reviewer tells you the movie stinks, he or she will go into some detail telling you exactly why. Reviewers go into similar detail when they explain why they gave a movie a four-star rating.

So you might read a long review dissecting a Patricia Cornwell novel made into a movie. But could you take the novel itself and write an assessment of what worked and what didn't? And are you teaching your students to assess their own writing?

It's not good enough to say "I liked it." We must help young writers know exactly what are the characteristics of good writing, how to spot them in a text, and how to revise effectively to improve those areas if they are deficient.

We hear a lot about "assessment informing instruction." For writing teachers, that just means that we read what our students write, see their weaknesses, and beef up our instructional presentations in those areas where they need help. We use our knowledge of effective writing also when we conference. Once you know what effective writing is, you can praise students when their writing demonstrates mastery of a concept. You can present craft lessons on areas where they are having problems and refer to those craft lessons as you conference during writing workshop.

It all begins with our being able to identify characteristics of effective writing. For the next six workouts, we will look at one of the most popular constructs in use by teachers today. It's Vicki Spandel's (Spandel & Stiggins, 1997, 2001)"six trait writing." Vicki, a master writing teacher and national presenter and author, has identified six traits of good writing, and her books and seminars show teachers how to assess those traits and to teach them using literature students enjoy. After reading about the six traits as presented here, if you want more information, get a copy of *Creating Writers* by Vicki Spandel and Richard J. Stiggins (2001).

In Your Writer's Notebook . . .

Think back to your own writing instruction in school. What do you remember about the ways you were taught to write? What specifically do you remember about the way your writing was assessed?

In Your Classroom Writer's Workshop . . .

Before you introduce the six traits (Spandel & Stiggins, 1997, 2001), let your class brainstorm what they think makes effective writing. You might let them begin by telling how they would assess a good hamburger, or movie, or rock song. When they have come up with a list, say, of what makes for a good hamburger and a bad hamburger, let them tell you what makes for a good piece of writing and a piece that just doesn't work. They will probably come up with some of the same things listed in the six traits.

The Six Traits
of Effective Writing:
#1—Ideas and Development

Have common sense and . . . stick to the point.

W. Somerset Maugham

In your writing you must go over your material in your mind, trying to find the focus, the perspective, the angle of vision that will make you see clearly the shape of whatever it is you are writing about. There has to be one point that is sharply in focus, and a clear grouping of everything else around it.

Rudolf Flesch

You settle down with a novel you've been looking forward to reading. It's a little hard to get into, but you forge ahead. And next thing you know, your mind is wandering. You catch yourself and return to your book, determined to at least finish the chapter. But the book doesn't hold your attention, and soon you're drifting again mentally.

Why does that happen? It could be any number of personal factors—or perhaps the fault of the writer. Perhaps the author never caught your attention in the first place with an engaging lead. Or perhaps the plot was hard to follow because of frequent digressions and wanderings from the main story. Or maybe the author never really helped you care about the characters by describing them and their interactions in a way that made them come alive in your mind.

Idea development includes all of these aspects. Vicki Spandel (2002) summarizes it in this way:

Ideas are the heart of any piece of writing. Ideas are all about information. In a strong creative piece, ideas paint a picture in the reader's mind. In an informational piece, strong ideas make difficult or complex information easy to understand. Good writing always makes sense. It always has a message or main point or story to tell. And it always includes carefully chosen details—those beyond-the-obvious bits of information that thoughtful, observant writers notice. (p. 2)

When authors excel at idea development, their writing is clear and to the point. The piece doesn't ramble; instead, it's focused on a primary story line or a manageable number of main ideas. The lead element entices you into the piece, and the writer has painted word pictures of the characters and setting, using the show, don't tell technique.

On the other hand, when idea development is lacking, you get the feeling that the piece is touching on many ideas but never developing any one. The writing is rambling and unfocused, perhaps because the author couldn't make up his mind about what he wanted to say or perhaps because he didn't have enough information to develop the piece properly.

In Your Writer's Notebook . . .

The writing trait of idea development is typically characteristic of writers who know how to focus on a main idea, who write about things they know and care about and thus choose interesting details to support their ideas. They don't write about love—they write about their mother, who sacrificed the cruise she had saved toward for years so they could buy their first car. They don't write about patriotism—they write about their World War II-veteran grandfather who shed a tear every time Old Glory passed by in a parade. A piece on the emotion of joy might ramble all over the place; a piece on the birth of your first child and what you experienced and how you felt will focus the reader on that one event.

Choose an abstraction—like love or freedom or unity or self-sacrifice or courage or joy—and write about it in a way that brings it to life. If you choose self-sacrifice, for instance, tell a story that exemplifies that quality but never mention the quality itself. Don't tell your readers that this person demonstrates self-sacrifice; show them.

In your classroom writer's workshop . . .

Take one of your writer's notebook entries to class to share with your students. But before you share, add some digressions and extraneous ideas. Chase a few rabbits—you know, like your students sometimes do in their prose. Tell your students what you have done, and then share your story. Ask them to point out the parts that ramble and get off topic. You might even print out two copies for them—one with the digressions and one without. They will be able to see how the more focused piece is easier to read. Then, in one-on-one conferences throughout the week, point out places where their writing moves off-topic in the same way yours did in the piece you shared with them.

The Six Traits of Effective Writing: #2—Organization

Ye shall know a poor literary structure by the sum of its ill-fitting parts.

David L. Carroll

Try to imagine this conversation. You run into a friend at a bookstore. She asked if you have read the latest novel by a popular author. You say you haven't.

"I just finished it," she says breathlessly, "and you just have to read it. It's wonderful. But mostly, it's so well organized."

Hard to imagine, isn't it? You've probably never heard someone raving about a book or recommending it because it was so well organized.

On other hand, you've probably heard people panning a book because they said it was hard to follow. What they were really saying was that it was disorganized. And when people tell you they kept reading far into the night because they couldn't put a book down, they may well have been telling you the book was well-organized.

Organization is the structure of a piece of writing. Writers who are adept at organization pull you into the story with a strong lead, then guide you through their narrative or their information, linking each event or idea together with effective transitions.

Organization is built on effective idea development—writers who know what they want to say and have narrowed the topic can then fit together the details to draw readers in. Well-organized pieces also move toward conclusions that bring closure to the story or the argument.

When the organization isn't effective, writers skip from idea to idea. There's little evidence of transition and no conclusion to wrap things up.

In education, there has been a movement during the last decade to address the problem of organization. Unfortunately, the cure for ineffective organization was worse than the disease. This writing panacea has been marketed under various names (you might be familiar with Power Writing and others like it). But whatever the name, they basically reduce writing to a paint-by-numbers kit. It's heavily prompt-driven, as are most misguided attempts to improve writing. Young writers are told that good writing consists of, for instance, a beginning statement, three points, and a conclusion that can be stated as a question.

These systems are right in addressing organization as one of the prime teaching points of writing. And they do provide a skeleton that helps some young writers get started and stay on track. But they should be viewed as a means to an end, not an end in themselves. They illustrate organization, and they model a type of organization. But the structure in these pieces comes to dominate the ideas themselves, and the writing is formulaic.

Good organization isn't so much following a pattern (like the famous five-paragraph essay) as it is paying attention. Writers who pay attention to craft revise with an eye toward organization. They frequently outline *after* a piece is finished to check for narrative flow, for ideas out of place, and for phrases or whole passages that can be cut out to remove detours that sidetrack their readers.

In Your Writer's Notebook . . .

Pick something you know how to do, something not too complex. It may be throwing a football, or scrambling eggs, or bathing your dog. Write out directions for someone who doesn't know how to do it like you do. Write it as a paragraph, not just a list of commands.

When you finish, note how you organized your paragraph (was it chronological? topical?) and underline your transitions.

In Your Classroom Writer's Workshop . . .

Ask any writing coach about the most difficult writing competency to teach. The answer will probably be organization. So relax—this isn't easy, and we're in it for the long haul. People have difficulty with organization in writing because they also have difficulty with organization in speaking.

Begin by pointing out the organization in stories and in informational text. Outline some short pieces to see what types of organization the author used. Use story maps to show students how writers incorporate elements like setting, problem, and resolution.

Let students outline editorials and letters to the editor in the newspaper. Let them list events in the order they happened in picture books. Make them aware of organization, and watch them begin to incorporate what they are learning into what they are writing.

The Six Traits of Effective Writing: #3—Voice

> Writing with no voice is dead, mechanical, faceless. It lacks any sound. Writing with no voice may be saying something true, important, or new; it may be logically organized; it may even be a work of genius. But it is as though the words came through some kind of mixer rather than being uttered by a person.
>
> *Peter Elbow*

> Voice separates writing that is not read from writing that is read. Voice gives a text concern, energy, humor, individuality, music, rhythm, pace, flow, surprise, believability. Voice includes the elements in writing that make it possible for printed marks on a page to become a single human being—a writer—speaking privately to another single human being—a reader.
>
> *Donald Murray*

Your church choir begins to sing, and you know instantly they are singing one of the choral works of Johann Sebastian Bach. You don't have to look at the church program or nudge the person sitting beside you on the pew. You just know; that is Bach's sound. And if your tastes run more into country than Baroque, could you ever fail to identify the unique music styling and voice of Willie Nelson?

You see Pudge Rodriguez step into the batter's box and settle in to prepare for a pitch. Even if Pudge was traded and is now wearing a different uniform, you know from watching his unique plate mannerisms just who's at the plate.

Or maybe you hear a new poem, but you'd pretty much be willing to bet the farm that the poet is Emily Dickinson or e.e. cummings or Robert Frost.

These poets and musicians—and even athletes—have an individuality in their approach. They leave their unique fingerprints on what they do and what they create. In writing, we call it voice. It's what separates a particular writer from all others.

There's no checklist of things to look for in identifying voice. Sometimes it involves word choice, sometimes vocabulary, sometimes a unique rhythm or meter. But it gives writing a unique sound you can recognize.

Can all writers express their individuality on paper? The answer is yes, but some key conditions have to prevail in that writer's life (or in a writing workshop environment, if the writer is in school):

1. Voice develops best in fluent writers. That is, people who write frequently and regularly, so that they are comfortable with the writing process.

2. Voice is encouraged when writers can identify what voice is—when they know voice when they read it or hear it, and when they have read books written by authors whose voice is strong.

3. Voice is largely a function of writing about what we know and what we care about. Writers of any age find it difficult to write with voice about something that isn't important to them or something they don't know a lot about. In school, writers who choose their own writing topics are more likely to write with voice.

4. Writers who feel free to take risks in their writing are the most likely to experiment with form and style and genre and approach in ways that encourage the development of voice.

In Your Writer's Notebook . . .

First, write a definition of voice in your writer's notebook. Write it as a letter to your class in a style, tone, and vocabulary appropriate to whatever grade you teach. Assume you were going to teach voice, not by explaining or illustrating it in class but by writing about it for your students. Or maybe you'd like to write the chapter on voice in your students' language arts book. However you see it, write for your students to explain the concept. Next day, take a writer's notebook day just to list writers whose voice you could identify. A good start to this might be to think of writers you'd be able to spot even if you were given a piece of their writing without a byline. List their names, and, if you can, write a sentence describing what's unique about their voice. Feel free to include poets, authors of children's literature, and even students in your class. If you can't do this from memory, pick up something written by someone you've just listed and read a little. Then try to write about the voice. This can be difficult, but remember that our job is teaching writing. And if we're going to help students understand voice, we must be able to articulate what it is. If you asked a football coach to describe the pass play that won the game, and he said, "Well, I thought it was pretty exciting but I couldn't really tell you exactly what was going on out there," you'd think the coach didn't know what he was doing. As teachers, we have to be able to articulate what we mean by voice and to give examples of it.

And if you'd really like to nail down the concept in your mind, try writing in the voice of a writer who's familiar to you. Maybe Walt Whitman or William Shakespeare or Ernest Hemingway—or perhaps Robert Munsch if you're a primary teacher who frequently reads this distinctively voiced Canadian writer to your students. For something that would really make an impact on your students, take something you have written and rewrite it in the voice of one or two other authors they would recognize.

In Your Classroom Writer's Workshop . . .

Work on a definition of voice with your students. Be sure they understand just what this trait involves. Collect books where the author writes with significant voice, and read selections from those books as examples of this writing trait in action.

When students write with voice, celebrate that in class. Sometimes, when students try something new, other areas of their writing suffer. Understanding the traits helps us to celebrate the trait we observe and to use a piece of writing as a good example of that trait in action, even if other traits are lacking. If the voice is strong, we can celebrate that and then talk with young writers about making their pieces even more effective by incorporating the other traits.

Writeaerobics Workout #19

The Six Traits of Effective Writing: #4—Word Choice

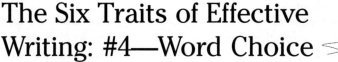

> Good writing is the least artificial, least labored, clearest, shapeliest and best carried out.
>
> It relates a very simple little incident in unpretentious language.
>
> It has the very rare merit of stopping when it is finished.
>
> It shows a freedom from adjective and superlatives, which is attractive, not to say seductive and let us remark, in passing, that one can seldom run his pen through an adjective without improving his manuscript.
>
> It has a singular aptness of language noticeable in it—denoting a shrewd facility of selecting just the right word for the service needed, as a general thing.
>
> It is a high gift. It is the talent which gives accuracy, grace and vividness in descriptive writing.
>
> Good writing's assets: unpretentiousness, simplicity of language and subject, a marked aptness and accuracy of wording, excellence of treatment, naturalness.
>
> *Mark Twain*

Twain's statement above, like many of his thoughts on writing, is a clear statement of the value of word choice. But he probably said it even better when he noted that the difference between the right word and the almost-right word "is the difference between lightning and a lightning bug."

Have you ever watched a bachelor shop, one who didn't like to cook? He runs into the supermarket, grabbing up items at random—anything to throw together for a meal. Then watch a chef select ingredients. The chef will spend longer picking out just the right squash than the non-cook will spend buying all his groceries. That's because the chef knows that all squashes aren't equal. The chef picks and prods and smells, looking for just the right ingredients for a dish he really cares about.

Word chefs (writers) are like that, too. Word choice is important to them. If a character is on the way from point *A* to point *B,* the writer cares about the verb that gets that character there. The writer could say he went, but that's too imprecise. A novice writer will add an adverb, and say the character went cautiously; the pro will say he crept, opting to use a more precise verb rather than a generic verb and an adverb.

Writers who excel at word choice use language that's just right for the piece in meaning, nuance, and tone. They write the type of prose and poetry that readers savor and want to read again.

No formula approach helps writers with word choice. Studying decontextualized vocabulary is practically meaningless. Writers known for effective word choice are themselves in love with language. They are avid readers. They love words and their sound. They enjoy playing with language. They have favorite writers and favorite passages they re-read until they almost have them memorized. They see words used in ways so effective that they look for ways to use those same words, or similar words, in writing of their own.

They are also writers committed to showing, not telling. When writers want to paint word pictures, they look for precise words that convey mental images. And it's those words, and those phrases, that we find memorable.

In Your Writer's Notebook . . .

As we indicated earlier in this book, sometimes writers just need to read the well-written works of others. Let's do that today, instead of writing in your notebook. Read the following passage from Sandra Cisneros' (1984) *The House on Mango Street:*

> Your abuelito is dead, Papa says early one morning in my room. Esta muerto, and then as if he just heard the news himself, crumples like a coat and cries, my brave Papa cries. I have never seen my Papa cry and I don't know what to do.
>
> I know he will have to go away, that he will take a plane to Mexico, all the uncles and aunts will be there, and they will have a black-and-white photo taken in front of the tomb with flowers shaped like spears in a white vase because this is how they send the dead away in that country. . . .
>
> My papa, his thick hands and thick shoes, who wakes up tired in the dark, who combs his hair with water, drinks his coffee, and is gone before we wake, today is sitting on my bed.
>
> And I think if my own Papa died what would I do. I hold my Papa in my arms. I hold and hold and hold him. (pp. 56–57)

Before you read the next paragraph, go back and re-read Cisneros' description of her father's reaction to his own father's death. Read it looking for instances of word choice that make the piece come alive.

Finished? Did you indicate some of the following?

1. Note the use of the Spanish phrases in an English piece. Those were the actual words her father used, and using them here gives authenticity to the piece.

2. She could have said her father threw himself across the bed. But notice her use of the word "crumples." It helps you picture exactly what her father did. And then, to really make the image vivid, she follows the strong verb with a simile: "like a coat." With several words of Spanish, a strong action verb, and a simile, she literally pulls you into the room with the girl and her Papa.

3. In the second paragraph, you have several words that give you a mental picture of a Mexican funeral. They are simple, but strong: "black-and-white photo," "flowers shaped like spears in a white vase," "how they send the dead away. . . ."

4. The third paragraph describes her father in striking phrases strung together in a long sentence. She could have said her father was a hard-working, blue-collar laborer. But you'd have no pictures. Note the word choice: "his thick hands and thick shoes, who wakes up tired in the dark, who combs his hair with water, drinks his coffee, and is gone before we wake. . . ."

5. Some writers might edit Ms. Cisneros' last paragraph to take out some of the holds. After all, doesn't she say the same thing over and over again? Of course she does. But she repeats the verb to indicate the duration of the embrace. Which is more powerful: I held my Papa for a very long time or "I hold my Papa in my arms. I hold and hold and hold him"?

The effectiveness of this short passage is the effectiveness of Sandra Cisneros' word choice. Analyze effective passages like this when you read and look for opportunities to apply the same principles when you write.

In Your Classroom Writer's Workshop . . .

Type out or photocopy a short passage like the one above for your class. The *House on Mango Street* (Cisneros, 1984) is full of such examples. Another good source is Carolyn Lesser's (1997) *Storm on the Desert*. You can also use several paragraphs from a novel you are reading or a short story your class enjoys. It's important to help students read like writers. Most non-writers will read a passage like the one above and find themselves touched or at least interested. But they won't know why. And the why, of course, is that the writer has involved them in the scene or description or story, frequently through effective word choice.

After you share a short passage that illustrates effective word choice, let students point out the writer's choices that bring the book to life for the reader. You might illustrate effective word choice in the passage you have chosen by substituting weak verbs and abstract nouns and then comparing that watered-down version with the author's version.

As with many other elements of the writing craft, we first help students to identify word choice in the writing of published authors. This helps them to be able to "talk writing," to see how authors use the elements of their craft. Then, you can begin to use the vocabulary they are developing as you teach and as you conference. Soon you will see instances of effective word choice (which you, of course, will identify and celebrate) in what they write.

The Six Traits of Effective Writing: #5—Sentence Fluency

> The best writers work with both long and short sentences. A gentle playfulness runs through the work of most good writers, a love for the language in which words hug and bump each other.
>
> *Roy Peter Clark*

Sentence fluency is flow, rhythm, and variety. It is well-crafted sentences. It is sentences that vary in structure. It is sentences that vary in length. It is sentences that relate to the sentences that precede and follow it.

Bottom line: Sentence fluency is everything the preceding paragraph isn't. Read the paragraph above one more time. It's correct, it's grammatical, and it contains the essential information a reader needs to know about sentence fluency. But it's dull. Every sentence has the same basic structure. Every independent-clause verb in the paragraph is the same: *is*. And one more thing—it's monotonous.

The key to sentence fluency is variety. Vary the verbs. Vary the beginnings. Vary the length of the sentences. Throw in a fragment occasionally, but use it intentionally for style. Use literary devices like alliteration and parallelism.

Spandel and Stiggins (2001) note that when writers manifest sentence fluency, "the writing has cadence, as if the writer hears the beat in his or her head" (p. 53).

Sentence fluency and voice are the most difficult of the six effective writing traits to teach. Writers don't really set out to write using sentence fluency. True, if they can identify the trait, they can edit later for sentence fluency. But only fairly experienced writers can deal with idea development, drafting, and sentence fluency at the same time. And that's true for fairly inexperienced writers of any age.

But even inexperienced writers can learn to appreciate sentence fluency, and to identify it. Then, as they revise and edit, they can look specifically for that trait. And if they see that all their sentences are pretty much the same length and pattern, they can edit for sentence variety.

Does that seem like a back-door, inadequate way to teach sentence fluency? It is. The best way to teach it goes back to something we talked about earlier: saturating the writer's life with beautiful language. Writers must read and be read to. They should memorize poetry. They should hear prose and poetry with rhythm and variety, like Edgar Allen Poe's *The Raven* and *The Bells*.

Fortunate indeed is the class whose teacher loves language, loves books, and loves to read out loud. That teacher marinates young writers in language. Day after day, they hear great prose and poetry.

Does that really work? Well, assume you had two children, and you wanted to teach both of them to bowl. Neither one had ever picked up a bowling ball before. But one had also never been in a bowling alley. The other had never been allowed to bowl, but every Thursday night she went bowling with her parents, who were in a bowling league. She just watched them bowl. She was in a bowling atmosphere for a couple of hours a week, though she never bowled herself.

Now you're going to try to teach both kids to bowl. Which will have the easier time learning the game? And if you had to bet which will be the better bowler after three lessons, who would you put your money on?

Obviously, the child who has been around bowlers and watched bowlers and listened to bowlers talk for several years has picked up a lot of information about bowling. She has been saturated in a bowling world. The sport will inevitably be easier to learn.

The same is true for writers. When writers have experienced great prose and poetry, those words and images and even rhythms are in their heads and in their hearts.

In Your Writer's Notebook . . .

Today, don't write. Instead, listen. Find some Shakespeare or Poe or any writer who is known for sentence fluency. Read something out loud and really listen to the rhythms. Notice how many ways good writers find to start sentences, and notice how easy it is to read out loud. Revel in the rhythm.

In Your Classroom Writer's Workshop . . .

Find a passage that illustrates sentence fluency in a book your students like. Type out that passage and let your students analyze it. Have them count the words in the sentences and analyze sentences for different structures. Let them notice how many ways sentences begin. Have them look for cadence, and let them read it out loud.

The Six Traits of Effective Writing: #6—Conventions

> If all the grammarians of the world were placed end to end, it would be a good thing.
>
> *Unknown*

One of the most hotly debated topics among writing teachers is the importance of conventions—grammar, spelling, punctuation, and proper word usage (to vs. too; affect vs. effect; different than vs. different from, etc.). Everyone agrees that the conventions are important. The issues are when do we teach them and how do we teach them.

One side says you teach conventions first, before writing. After all, how can you write until you understand basic grammar, so that you can use proper grammar in your writing? So you decontextualize spelling and grammar and teach those subjects, so that students can master them for use in their writing.

Another side says that approach is all wrong. Just let students write, so they will be comfortable with the act of writing and will see themselves as writers. The conventions will come as they become fluent writers and readers.

Who's right?

Both, and neither. As with most complex issues, the truth lies somewhere between. Teaching grammar apart from writing may produce students who do well on grammar tests, but it doesn't carry over into writing. So we're left with that old teacher's mantra: "But we covered that!" Students who passed the participle test with flying colors can't seem to use them effectively when they write.

On the other side, some teachers just hope that students who are fluent writers will just intuitively use correct grammar and spelling. Students in their classes enjoy writing and see themselves as writers, but sometimes their grammar is atrocious. Their teachers keep hoping that their grammar will magically improve, but often it just doesn't.

One approach combines the best of both worlds: teaching grammar in a writing environment. We begin with writing, not grammar. But we constantly talk about grammar the way real writers see it. That is, that correct grammar is something we do as a service to the reader. People who build highways don't get creative with stop signs. They are all the same color and the same shape. A round green stop sign would just confuse drivers. By the same token, nobody ever reads a best-seller and raves about the grammar. On the other hand, variances in grammar or spelling are distracting to readers.

Writers see the elements of grammar as a tool they use in telling stories and passing along information. Ask a student what an adjective is. If the student says it's a word that modifies a noun, she has been taught grammar decontextualized from writing. But if she is asked what an adjective is, and she replies, "An adjective is a word writers use to help readers picture a person or an object," that student has been taught grammar as a tool for writers.

So do we teach about active and passive voice, and verbals, and adverbs? Of course. But some teachers, whenever they talk about parts of speech, begin their sentences with "Writers use . . ." So they're constantly saying writers use adjectives to . . ., and writers use gerunds to . . ., and writers use the active voice to . . .

Effective writing teachers show students that a paper can be technically and grammatically perfect and still have poor organization or no voice or ineffective word choice. Good use of conventions does not make effective writing. On the other hand, a piece can be really good and lose its effectiveness because of poor conventions. When conventions are taught in the context of editing and preparation for publication, young writers come to view them just as professional writers do.

In Your Writer's Notebook . . .

Go back in your notebook and find a piece you're fairly satisfied with. Something you consider to be well written. Today, instead of writing something, analyze the grammar in what you wrote. Highlight all nouns in one color, all verbs in another. Circle adjectives and participle phrases. Underline adverbs.

Now, go back and look at your nouns. Are they vague and general or concrete and specific? Are your verbs strong? Look at verbs with adverbs. Did you use a weak verb and an adverbial modifier when you should have used a stronger verb instead?

In Your Classroom Writer's Workshop . . .

If you made any changes in your own writing as a result of your grammatical analysis, share that with your students.

Type out a passage from a book your students really like. Be sure to leave lots of room between lines. Let your students do what you just did to your own piece of writing. Show them, from a piece of writing they already acknowledge to be effective (like one of the Harry Potter books), how writers use grammar to communicate effectively.

For additional grammar practice, take a passage from a novel students enjoy and insert errors in grammar and conventions. This gives your students practice in finding errors in grammar, spelling, and punctuation, but it also shows them how distracting it can be to readers to find such mistakes.

Writeaerobics Workout #22

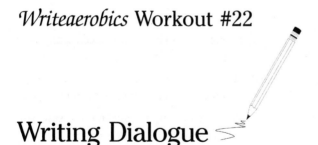

Writing Dialogue

> Listen to the way people really talk. If your characters sound real, the rest is easy.
>
> *David Eddings*

> I don't have a very clear idea of who the characters are until they start talking.
>
> *Joan Didion*

Dialogue—along with effective use of description can make writing come alive. Descriptive writing paints a picture in the reader's mind. Dialogue makes characters sound real through memorable voices and real-world-sounding conversations that give a ring of authenticity to writing.

How do you learn to write good dialogue? Just listen; it's going on around you every day. Listen like a writer to the conversations at lunch or in your car or at the checkout stand in the supermarket. Listen for content and phrasing and word choice. In your writer's notebook, try reproducing those conversations, or at least snatches of them. Don't worry about telling a story using dialogue. Just reproduce some "slices of life" in conversation.

Let's say you're behind a couple in the express lane of the supermarket. They are complaining about the slowness of the checkout person. And it doesn't take long for them to jump from the fact that she's slow . . . to their supposition that she's stupid . . . to their conjecture that most teen-agers who work in grocery stores are equally clueless . . . to what's this generation coming to anyway?

Listen to them. If you were a non-writer this would be eavesdropping. Writers call it research. Listen for specific phrases, watch for mannerisms and body language, and pay attention to the way "your characters" are dressed and how they look. Then, as soon as you can, find some paper and write the dialogue you've just heard. Don't worry about having a beginning or ending. Just get this "slice of life" down on paper.

You only need a few basics to write engaging dialogue:

1. You need a good story to start with, one that can be embellished by dialogue that makes the characters come alive.

2. You need to know how to handle the mechanics of dialogue (see any good grammar and usage book for the common rules of punctuating quotations).

3. You need to know how to write natural-sounding conversation, a skill you will pick up from observing how good writers use dialogue and from "listening like a writer" to real conversations.

In Your Writer's Notebook . . .

Take a few days just to record the conversations around you. Tom Chiarella (1998), in his book *Writing Dialogue*, tells you how to eavesdrop like a writer:

> There are certain places where you can't avoid overhearing conversations. Subways are super (but notice how hard it is to hear, and notice how little people really say there). The baggage carousel at the airport . . . is one of my favorite spots. [At airports] you can put up a newspaper and lean back to hear the guy in the row of seats behind you apologizing to his children for leaving them to go skiing. Or you can lean against a wall and listen to a family waiting for one grandmother or the other to step through the gate. People tend to resolve things at airports, or try to, if only temporarily.
>
> There are other nice spots. Diners, with their back-to-back booths. Parks. Barbecue joints. Movie theaters, before the show. Lines at the bank. Baseball games. Airport limousines. Hotel lobbies. Convenience stores. Oil change places. Museums. Post offices.
>
> How do you do it? Take one step closer. Lean in slightly. Make yourself as quiet as you can and stare straight ahead. [Steal] the words from the air around you. (p. 14)

In Your Classroom Writer's Workshop . . .

Share Bill Martin, Jr. and John Archambault's (1985) picture book *The Ghost-Eye Tree* with your class—no matter what grade level you teach. High schoolers will enjoy this wonderful tale as much as primaries do. Almost the entire story is told in dialogue. After you have read the story, assign someone to play the roles of the boy, his sister, and Mr. Cowlander. Someone else can be the narrator. Note that in addition to the dialogue, the story also includes internal monologue—what the character is thinking. Another good way to look at both dialogue and internal monologue is through cartoons. Photocopy some cartoons from the Sunday paper (*Classic Peanuts* is especially good for this exercise). Point out to your students that cartoons are pure dialogue and internal monologue, but the narration is carried by the pictures. Have your students write the story of the cartoon just as they would if it appeared as a short story in a book. The pictures will be reflected in the narrative, and the words in the speech bubbles become the actual dialogue in the story. This helps young writers see how authors use dialogue.

Writeaerobics Workout #23

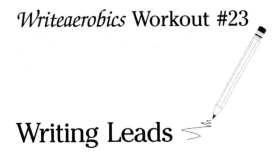

Writing Leads

> Always grab the reader by the throat in the first paragraph, sink your thumbs into his windpipe in the second, and hold him against the wall until the tag line.
>
> *Paul O'Neil*

> What's so hard about the first sentence is that you're stuck with it. Everything else is going to flow out of that sentence. And by the time you've laid down the first two sentences, your options are all gone.
>
> *Joan Didion*

The word "lead" was coined by journalists to describe the first paragraph of a news or feature story, since its function was to grab the attention of readers and "lead" them into the rest of the story. During the 1990s, the journalists' term was appropriated by teachers as a good way to help students see the importance and function of opening sentences.

A lead can actually mean two different things, depending on how you want to use the term. The traditional journalistic use was the first sentence of a news or feature story. The journalistic convention is to limit the first paragraph to only once sentence in the interest of readability (assuming the reader might be turned off by multiple lines of type), so in journalism a lead is the first sentence, which is also typically the first paragraph.

But *lead* can also be used in another way: as the opening element of a piece of writing. That would include not only the first paragraph, but also the next few paragraphs that followed it. For example, you might be writing a piece about your poodle Pompidou and why he is such an important part of your family. Perhaps you begin your piece with an anecdote about how Pompi sleeps in bed with you and your spouse, his head on a pillow between you. That anecdote might be three paragraphs long. The lead in this case would really be a *lead element* of several paragraphs. Your goal would be to intrigue your readers with this anecdote about your dog, to draw them into the rest of the piece.

So how do you write a good lead?

Good question, and one with no answer. If you look in books on writing, you'll find lots of information on writing leads. Authors will tell you why leads are so important, and they will give you lots of types of leads. You might read a 25-page chapter on leads, more information than you ever knew existed on the topic. But when you finish those 25 pages, you'll note that the writer didn't answer the basic question: How do you write a good lead?

A Supreme Court justice said he couldn't define pornography, he just knew it when he saw it. The same is true for leads. Writers can give you all kinds of examples of good leads. They can give you the major categories of leads. But when it's all said and done, you have to face the blank page yourself.

And while there's no formula for writing a good lead, you should definitely do two things if you want to improve your leads:

First, study the categories or types of leads. That brings us back to the books we mentioned above, the ones we said couldn't teach you to write a lead. They can't, but they can help you impose some order on the mystifying world of leads. (See Workshop 6, "Crafting Engaging Leads: Great Beginnings for Good Writing," in *Absolutely Write! Teaching the Craft Elements of Writing* [Thomason & York, 2002].) Those categories will include anecdotal leads that begin with a story, descriptive leads that begin with setting a scene or describing a person, leads that begin with a summary statement of what the article is about, leads that feature dialogue, question leads—the list is long, and frequently overlapping, like the anecdotal lead that features a lot of dialogue.

And second, become a lead-noticer and even perhaps a lead collector. In other words, read like a writer. Notice how writers begin their stories or articles. Look for leads that fit into the categories listed above or leads that represent new categories. You might even want to collect your favorite leads and file them away. If they're short (like "Call me Ishmael,") you might just copy them into your book. If they're longer or really represent a lead element of several paragraphs, you might want to photocopy them, cut them out, and paste them in.

One last piece of advice: Don't stare at your paper forever trying to come up with a good lead. The more you learn about leads, sometimes, the more anemic yours look. The solution for many writers, if the lead doesn't come soon, is to write something like this: "Here's my lead for the piece about my dog. I'll tell a story that illustrates how he thinks he's a human." Then just go on. You know what your piece is about, and you know you will write an anecdotal lead. So skip the lead and write the rest of the piece. By the time you finish, you'll probably know what you want your lead to be about. It'll be the first thing your reader reads, but it may well be the last thing you wrote. Take, for instance, the preface to this book, which is sort of like a lead for the entire book. Though logically you might think the author wrote it first, it was actually written last. At the beginning, the author only had a vague idea of what he wanted to say. But by the time the book was almost finished, he knew exactly how it needed to be introduced.

In Your Writer's Notebook . . .

Look back over some of the pieces you have written. First, look for the type(s) of approaches you tend to be taking to leads. Then, try something different. Maybe you want to drop the reader immediately into the middle of the action instead of setting a scene or building up to it. Or maybe you've written an anecdotal lead and you want to try a descriptive lead instead. Don't rewrite the whole piece—just the lead. That may be one sentence or one paragraph, or two or three. The goal of this writer's notebook exercise is just to try some different lead approaches and see if you think they improve what you have already written.

In Your Classroom Writer's Workshop . . .

For this workshop, see appendix B, "The Escaped Python Story." Use this with your students, and then do your own. It's easy to come up with a basic set of story facts to allow students to play with leads.

Point of View: The
Perspective of the Narrator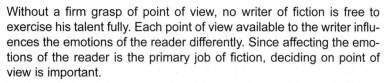

> Without a firm grasp of point of view, no writer of fiction is free to exercise his talent fully. Each point of view available to the writer influences the emotions of the reader differently. Since affecting the emotions of the reader is the primary job of fiction, deciding on point of view is important.
>
> *Sol Stein*

John Scieszka did more to communicate the power of point of view in writing than any textbook ever could.

For years, children grew up hearing The Three Little Pigs told from the standpoint of an "omniscient" storyteller—someone outside the story who knows what each character is thinking, feeling, and doing . . . and why.

Then Scieszka told the three pigs tale from the standpoint of the wolf in *The True Story of the Three Little Pigs* (1989). And suddenly, young writers in classrooms throughout the nation saw what effects a change in point of view could have.

The point of view is the place from which the reader views a story. If you imagine your story as a movie, then viewpoint is where you place the camera. Usually the camera is inside a character's head, looking out through his eyes. He is the viewpoint character and the camera records what he sees, smells, hears, and tastes. But the viewpoint is an emotional camera, not a mechanical one, and when you choose a viewpoint you are also choosing what the viewpoint character feels, thinks, and believes.

Writers have used various points of view to tell their stories:

- The all-knowing (omniscient) point of view (see above).

- First person point of view: The narrator is a character in the story and uses I, me, and so on to refer to himself or herself. Readers will know only what the narrator does, thinks, or feels.

- Third-person limited point of view: The narrator is outside the story, but tells the story chiefly from the main character's point of view.

Writers should be aware of the point of view in what they are reading and aware of how they can sometimes revitalize their pieces by changing points of view. Sometimes doing what Scieszka did and telling your story from a different point of view can bring it to life for the reader.

In Your Writer's Notebook . . .

Rewrite a well-known story from a different point of view—Cinderella from the perspective of a wicked stepsister or the prince, or one of the Harry Potter vignettes featuring the Dursleys from the point of view of Dudley Dursley.

In Your Classroom Writer's Workshop . . .

1. Make a point of view chart, with titles of books written in a vertical column on the left and types of point of view written in a horizontal column across the top. Take some of your class favorites and let your young writers categorize them.

2. Copy the leads included in appendix B of this book. Though that section is presented to help with lead-writing, your writers can also go through the various types of leads presented and identify the point of view in each book.

3. Read something you wrote as a writing application where you wrote a familiar story from a different point of view.

4. Let your writers practice changing the point of view in a paragraph you supply.

Writeaerobics Workout #25

Revision: How
Writers View the Process

> By the time I am nearing the end of a story, the first part will have been
> reread and altered and corrected at least one hundred and fifty times.
> I am suspicious of both facility and speed. Good writing is essentially
> rewriting. I am positive of this.
>
> *Roald Dahl*

Only writers enjoy revision. Non-writers dread it; they see no purpose in it; they see
it as drudgery. How many times have you heard one of your students whine, "Do we
have to revise this?"

Writers, on the other hand, see revision in a totally different light. To them, it's an
integral part of the writing process. It's what takes an OK piece and turns in into an
unforgettable piece of prose or poetry.

Since writers see revision in such a different way, today we'll just hear from some
writers whose work you may have read. Read what they have to say about revision,
and perhaps use it as a springboard to revise your own thinking on revision:

> The beautiful part of writing is that you don't have to get it right the first
> time, unlike, say, a brain surgeon. You can always do it better, find the
> exact word, the apt phrase, the leaping simile.
>
> *Robert Cormier*

> I don't think anything I've written has been done in under six or eight
> drafts.
>
> *E. L. Doctorow*

> All the best cutting is done when one is sick of the writing.
>
> *John Fowles*

Write it out as verbose as you want. Have verbal diarrhea. Then cut the unnecessary words, but keep the plot. Then rewrite and cut again. Then rewrite and cut again. After three times, you have something.

David Mamet

I do not choose the right word. I get rid of the wrong one.

A. E. Housman

Rewriting is when playwriting really gets to be fun. In baseball you only get three swings and you're out. In rewriting, you get almost as many swings as you want and you know, sooner or later, you'll hit the ball.

Neil Simon

I have rewritten—often several times—every word I have ever published. My pencils outlast their erasers.

Vladimir Nabokov

The main rule of a writer is never to pity your manuscript. If you see something is no good, throw it away and begin again.

Isaac Beshevis Singer

Write freely and as rapidly as possible and throw the whole thing on paper. Never correct or rewrite until the whole thing is down. Rewrit[ing] in process is usually found to be an excuse for not going on.

John Steinbeck

In Your Writer's Notebook . . .

Read today's quotes again, and then think back on how you have always viewed revision. Do you look at it like these writers do? Why or why not? Write about your experience with revision and how you feel about it.

In Your Classroom Writer's Workshop . . .

Use some of today's quotes in a craft lesson on revision—not showing students how and when and where to revise, but talking about the philosophy of revision and how writers view it. Point out that revision is something writers do for their readers because they want their manuscript to be as good as it can be. Note that before you leave for school every morning, you engage in revision—of yourself. You put on clean clothes and brush your teeth and comb your hair. Girls may apply makeup. It's all personal revision—because we know we'll be going out in public. Contrast that with what you might do if you were staying at home all day Saturday and knew you wouldn't be seeing anyone. You'd do a lot less personal revision. And so, when you are just writing, you don't think so much of revision. But if it's something you plan for others to read and enjoy, you concentrate much more on revision.

How Revision Works, and Why It's Hard to Teach

If you want to be read more than once, do not hesitate to blot often.

Horace

Blot out, correct, insert, refine.

Enlarge, diminish, interline.

Be mindful, when invention fails,

To scratch your head, and bite your nails.

Jonathan Swift

In Workout #25, you saw how writers look at revision. Perhaps you wish you or your young writers could see revision in the same way. The dread with which many of us face revision, though, is a natural outgrowth of our own experience with writing in school.

Here's what has happened: Schools look for writing improvement. And of course, writing improvement comes about as the result of revision. So non-writers want to put a lot of emphasis on revision. And for decades now, non-writers have determined the course of writing instruction. Writers also honor revision—that's obvious from the authors quoted in Workout #25. But here's the difference: They are writers. Only writers will understand revision or be motivated to revise.

So if we want young writers to understand revision and its techniques and to choose to revise their work, we don't begin by teaching revision. We begin by helping them become fluent writers. There are several steps to effective revision:

First, writers must write regularly, so that writing becomes a habit and they become comfortable with the writing process—that's fluency.

Next, writers must come to read like writers—to see writing they enjoy as models for what they can do in their own pieces.

Then, writers must be given the opportunity to share their work with others through oral reading and published pieces. It's in that context that we introduce revision.

After all, revision is audience-centered. If we were just writing for ourselves, we wouldn't need to revise. There would be no need to clean up conventions—for the same reason you typically don't clean house if you know you won't be having visitors. And there would be no need to rewrite for clarity or to help the reader visualize what we are writing about if we knew nobody would see the piece but us.

So revision is just a common-sense reaction to imminent publication. And you don't revise everything you write, just like you don't "revise" your appearance if you know you won't be leaving your home on Saturday. You'll wear a pair of grubby sweats and your old college t-shirt, and you might not even comb your hair, much less shave or put on makeup. But if you're going out that day—the imminent audience—you take great pains to look good.

Revision is a high-level skill. Writing is one thing, but re-thinking what you have written and playing with different approaches—that takes writing maturity. And writing maturity comes only with writing. In Cecil B. DeMille's *The Ten Commandments*, Pharaoh declares to Moses his unwillingness to change his mind with these words: "What I have written, I have written." And he thereby became the spiritual godfather of millions of future writers who would see no reason to change what they had put in print.

The willingness to revise is more caught than taught. Those who have learned how to appreciate revision have typically learned it from exposure to a writer, from watching revision going on. They learned revision in the same way people learn to "revise" as they cook. Most of us learned to cook at the elbow of our mother or some other relative. We watched as she cooked, perhaps following a recipe or just combining the ingredients of a favorite recipe. As she cooked, she tasted, looking ahead to when her family would eat the dish she was preparing. She added salt or pepper or some other spice, revising as she went. And we came to understand culinary "revision" as a normal part of cooking.

As teachers, we foster revision by revising ourselves in front of our students. Let them see not only product, but also process. When you bring something you have written, bring your original copy, too. Let them see how much changing and marking out you do. Occasionally, after you share a piece you have written, ask your class, "Would you like to see this the first time I wrote it?" Show your young writers your first and second, maybe even third, versions, before you ever got to the product you eventually shared with the class.

You can't rush revision with young writers. You can teach lessons on it, but they will never choose to revise until they see it as a normal part of the writing process. . . . and until they are motivated by the opportunity to share their writing with an audience.

In Your Writer's Notebook . . .

Choose a piece you have written in your writer's notebook. Something you like and wouldn't mind revising. Pick one thing to work on. You don't have to rewrite everything—just work on the beginning or the end, or insert some dialogue or internal monologue, or bring something to life through the show, don't tell principle.

In Your Classroom Writer's Workshop . . .

They need to know the difference between copyediting and revising. Copyediting is looking for grammar, spelling, punctuation, and usage errors. It's important, but it's not revising. You can teach this by warm-up exercises where you give students a sentence with several editing errors. First, you can copyedit the sentence for mechanical errors; then, revise it to improve the writing. Here are two examples:

Start with this:	I seen the sky and it was really quiet beauteful.
Copyedited:	I saw the sky, and it was really quite beautiful.
Revised:	Shades of burnt orange and gold spilled across the afternoon sky.

Start with this:	My littel brother ben was so angry he culdn't hardly stand it.
Copyedited:	My little brother Ben was so angry he could hardly stand it.
Revised:	Ben kicked his wastebasket and stomped out of the room, slamming his bedroom door behind him.

Notice that these simple exercises take only a few minutes and they teach grammar, spelling, punctuation, copyediting, and revision. If you revise the original sentence using copyediting marks instead of just rewriting the sentence, you are also teaching the effective use of those marks. And you constantly reinforce the meaning of revision—and the techniques of revision—when you extend editing to revision.

You can also tie this craft lesson to literature by taking a well-written sentence from a book your students enjoy and substituting weak verbs, abstract nouns, and wordy phrases. After you have a weaker version of the author's sentence, insert grammar and punctuation errors. Your students can copyedit for the errors and then revise the sentence to make it more effective. Then you can show them the author's original sentence, and they can compare their revision with what the author originally wrote.

Writeaerobics Workout #27

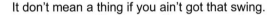

Feel the
Beat . . . Then Write

It don't mean a thing if you ain't got that swing.

Duke Ellington

In the movie *Hardball*, the story of a down-on-his-luck gambler who ends up managing a baseball team of kids from the projects in Chicago, a young pitcher never takes off his headphones. He's listening to only one rap song, over and over. But he keeps on mowing down the other team's batters, one after the other.

And then an opposing coach appeals to the rulebook and forces him to remove the headphones. When the music is no longer in his head, he is no longer effective as a pitcher. (In case you want to know what happens, his teammates eventually started rapping the lyrics in the field so he could successfully get back into his game.)

Some writers are like that—they enjoy listening to music as they write. Is it just for background noise? Maybe. But music can also call up memories and feelings, transport us to another place and time, and set a tone or mood. Music can also provide a cadence, a rhythm, that can be reflected in our prose or poetry.

Although some writers prefer a given composer, like Mozart or Bach, or anything from a given musical style, like jazz or blues, other writers like a specific song to get them started when they write. The following three writers (quoted in Clark, 2002) each have their favorite songs for writing:

Jonathan Dube of MSNBC.com listens to the Rolling Stones' "Start Me Up":

> Listening to this song is like getting a shot of adrenaline in the arm—again and again and again. I can feel it moving through my body each time Keith Richards strokes his guitar, flooding me with bursts of energy.

> This song motivates, awakens, energizes, inspires. If you're facing the wall of writer's block, this will give you what you need to break through it. It really does start you up. (p. 10)

Stephanie Stockett of Black Entertainment Television, listens to "Back in One Piece" by Aaliyah and DMX:

> I always choose a hip hop or R&B song to move me before I write. I'm suggesting this song because it is both. In the song, featured on the "Romeo Must Die" movie soundtrack, the song beats behind the words are what motivate me. And hip hop, with its racy lyrics and question-able subject matter, reminds me to always write my truths.

Journalism professor Bill Sutley of Auburn University listens to Etta James singing "At Last":

> Even though this is a love song with lyrics that sometimes don't make sense ("My heart was wrapped up in clover"), it just gets me in a mood to write. I'm not entirely sure why.
>
> From a psychological standpoint, I've come to believe strongly that I far prefer being in the position of "having written" than facing a blank computer screen. This song's repetitive "at last" hook reminds me that I will get something written "at last," if I plant my butt down in a chair and start to write. The song makes a good post-writing serenade as well.

In Your Writer's Notebook . . .

So try it. Put some music on before you write, and listen for a few minutes. Then just write and see what comes. If you can't write while vocalists are singing, try something instrumental.

In Your Classroom Writer's Workshop . . .

Lots of teachers use music in their writing workshop. Scott Beesley, a fourth-grade teacher in Las Vegas, Nevada, who uses music in writing every day, suggests that you begin with Gustav Holst's "The Planets," a suite that includes a motif for each planet. Each will call up different images for your students. If they have trouble writing while music is playing, have your students close their eyes and listen for a few minutes. Then ask, "Where did that music take you?" Before they write, just let them talk about images that came to mind—people or historical eras or places. Then, let them listen to the music again. And then, write. If they want to listen to the music while they are writing, let it continue to play.

Writeaerobics Workout #28

Bringing It in for a Landing: Writing Endings

> Begin at the beginning, keep going until you get to the end, and then stop.
>
> *Lewis Carrol*
>
> *Alice's Adventures in Wonderland*

> I always know the ending; that's where I start.
>
> *Toni Morrison*

> The story ending is the icing on the cake, the neat knot that carefully ties up the story strands so that the reader can put the story aside with a sense of satisfaction.
>
> *Barbara Mariconda*

Engaging leads are difficult to write, but perhaps not so difficult as endings. That's because students typically pay more attention to the way a story begins than the way it ends, and also because we spend more time teaching openings than closings. So we get endings like these:

- That's the end of my story.
- And then it ended. The end.
- I hope you enjoyed my story. That's all.
- I woke up and found it was only a dream.

But just as lead-writing is a skill young authors can learn, so is the crafting of satisfying endings. As with lead-writing, there are several stages in developing this skill: First, young writers must be made aware of endings and the various ways authors end stories and expository pieces. Then, they must become students of the craft of endings, and begin to practice the techniques they have been studying in their own pieces. They must continue to experiment with various types of endings until they begin to consistently apply what they are learning in their own work.

Endings are difficult, partly because we pay less attention to them than we do to beginnings and partly because there are fewer "ending types" than there are lead types. There are no "standard" endings. Therefore, writers must pay close attention to good endings until they get a feel for what a good ending is. Here is a list, by no means exhaustive, of some approaches to endings:

1. The surprise ending. The writer has hidden something from the reader not revealed until the last few sentences. An excellent example of this is Martin and Archambault's (1986) *White Dynamite and Curly Kidd.* In this picture book, the narrator, a would-be rodeo bull rider, is presumed to be a boy. Readers find out at the very end that the narrator is a girl. Barbara Abercrombie's (1990*) Charlie Anderson* is another good picture-book example of an ending surprise.

2. The circular ending returns to something or someone introduced in the lead. Sometimes it completes a story that was begun in the opening paragraphs. Look at Natalie Babbit's (1975) *Tuck Everlasting* for an example of this technique. The book both begins and ends with Winnie watching the frog.

3. Dialogue endings conclude with characters talking with each other about the action of the story, as in J. K. Rowling's (1999) *Harry Potter and the Chamber of Secrets*:

> "Your aunt and uncle will be proud, though, won't they?" said Hermione as they got off the train and joined the crowd thronging toward the enchanted barrier. "When they hear what you did this year?"
>
> "Proud?" said Harry. "Are you crazy? All those times I could've died, and I didn't manage it? They'll be furious."
>
> And together they walked back through the gateway to the Muggle world. (p. 341)

4. Insight endings occur when the main character comes to an understanding of why something happened or resolves to complete some action in the future. Rebecca Wells' (1996) *Divine Secrets of the Ya-Ya Sisterhood* ends in this way:

> For Siddalee Walker, the need to understand had passed, at least for the moment. All that was left was love and wonder. (p. 356)

5. Sometimes stories end with poetry or song recited or sung by an important character, or overheard by a character. The verses recited or heard will typically have been introduced somewhere else in the story and are re-introduced at the end to establish a mood or a feeling. Gloria Houston (1994) does this at the end of her historical fiction novel *Mountain Valor:*

Valor immediately followed her family to the house and sat on the porch as they talked long into the spring twilight. But she was silent, for the she listened to hear someone come riding across the meadow whistling.

"The gypsy rover came over the hill,
And down through the green wood so shady.
He whistled and sang 'til the green wood rang,
And he won the heart of a lady." (p. 236)

The five ending types just mentioned only scratch the surface. Many endings will combine two or more of these types. As with all other elements of writing craft, writers pay attention to what they read. Most readers will finish a novel, even one they enjoyed, and never notice how the writer crafted the ending. They will probably remember what happened at the end, but not the way in which the writer brought the story in for a landing. But writers—even young writers—notice these craft elements. Most people who eat at an excellent restaurant will only remember how much they enjoyed the food. But chefs who eat there notice textures and ingredients and unique combination of flavors. In the same way, as you introduce your young writers to ways authors craft endings, they will begin to notice the way writers conclude their pieces and to copy those ending techniques when they write.

In Your Writer's Notebook . . .

Set aside some pages in your writer's notebook to copy endings you like from books you read. Try to categorize them as best you can. This will be difficult, because many won't fit your categories. Don't worry about that—make up a new category. As you become more and more aware of endings, you will begin to see that there are some fairly common ways writers end stories, narratives, and informational pieces.

Pick a few pieces from your writer's notebook and re-work the endings. If possible, share them with your class, showing them why you thought those pieces needed more work on their endings and how you went about re-crafting the ending.

In Your Classroom Writer's Workshop . . .

If you're serious about teaching endings, you'll also get the additional benefit of boosting your state writing achievement scores. Good endings are seldom encountered by those who score papers. You can improve endings by:

1. Doing craft lessons on endings to increase awareness of how writers conclude stories.

2. Collecting endings students like on a chart displayed for your young writers to see. Beginning a class listing of ending types like the one above, one to which you can add new types as students discover them; and

3. Celebrating creative endings as your students experiment with new approaches in writing workshop.

Vivid Verbs:
Bringing Life to Writing

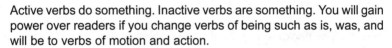

Active verbs do something. Inactive verbs are something. You will gain power over readers if you change verbs of being such as is, was, and will be to verbs of motion and action.

Gary Provost

Ask any writer what's the most important element in lively prose. The answer you'll get, no matter how many writers you ask, is the same: verbs.

Verbs give life to writing; they are the energy in any sentence. And the key to effective verbs is a concept we've already looked at: show, don't tell. Generally speaking, verbs are weak when they aren't specific or when they rely too much on accompanying adverbs.

Good writers wouldn't choose the verb *look* if they really meant stare or gaze or peek or peer or gawk. And it only compounds the problem if you write look intently instead of stare.

Notice how each of these weak, imprecise verbs is improved by substituting its more precise cousin:

Weak: Susan ate her lunch.

Stronger: Susan gobbled her lunch.

Weak: The coach threw the ball to Jose and told him he was the new pitcher.

Stronger: The coach tossed (or maybe flipped) the ball to Jose and told him he was the new pitcher.

Weak: Tigers hunt their prey.

Stronger: Tigers stalk their prey.

Weak: "I never want to see you again!" Sandra said angrily.

Stronger: "I never want to see you again!" Sandra snarled.

Writers also try to use the active voice unless the context demands a passive construction. ("Voice" indicates whether the subject acts or is acted upon, whether the subject is the doer of the action or the receiver of the action.)

This is active: Billy hit the ball.

This is passive: The ball was hit. Or: The ball was hit by Billy.

Note how switching to the active voice saves words (active sentences are shorter than passives) and makes sentences more lively and immediate:

Passive: The test was taken by the students.

Active: The students took the test.

Passive: The books were placed on the table by Sean.

Active: Sean placed the books on the table.

Even better (because the verb is more specific): Sean dropped the books on the table.

Begin to look for strong, active verbs in the books you read. As you look for strong verbs, you will come to appreciate their power and use them more yourself in your own writing.

In Your Writer's Notebook . . .

In her classic *Writing Down the Bones*, Natalie Goldberg (1986) suggests an exercise that can give writers a new perspective on verbs: Fold a piece of paper in half vertically. On one side, list ten nouns. On the other side, think of an occupation, like teaching (or carpentry or medicine or law enforcement). List ten verbs that go with that position. For teaching, for instance, you might list: grade, lecture, coach (as in coaching writing), observe, etc.

Then open the page. You will have a column of nouns on one side and a column of verbs on the other. Try joining the nouns to the verbs to see what new combinations you get, and then finish the sentences, casting the verbs in whatever tense you need them to be in. You'll get some interesting noun/verb combinations.

Also in your writer's notebook, set aside a few pages for great verbs you find in your reading. Copy the sentence with the expressive verb directly into your book. Be sure to put the title of the book and the page number, because you'll probably come back to these pages as you put together craft lessons on verbs.

In Your Classroom Writer's Workshop . . .

Have your students do the same exercise (writing down sentences with strong verbs) in their writer's notebooks. The verbs they write down will begin appearing in their writing. Also, it will help your young writers appreciate the power of strong verbs, a necessary first step toward using stronger verbs.

Also, you can make students more aware of verbs with three-minute strong-verbs craft lessons scattered throughout the day for several weeks. Just give them a sentence with a weak verb and let them brainstorm how it could be strengthened. Be sure, as they share suggestions, to point out how the various verbs all add a different shade of meaning to the sentence. Here are some weak-verb sentences to get you started:

- He ate three hamburgers.
- John walked down the road. (John was lazy.)
- John walked down the road. (John was in a hurry.)
- John walked down the road. (John was trying to avoid being seen.)
- John walked down the road. (John was happy.)

Writeaerobics Workout #30

Can We Teach
Students to Write Creatively?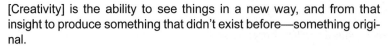

> [Creativity] is the ability to see things in a new way, and from that insight to produce something that didn't exist before—something original.
>
> *Bill Moyers*

> Being creative is seeing the same thing as everybody else but thinking of something different.
>
> *Anonymous*

You frequently hear people lament the lack of creativity in student writing. And no wonder. High-stakes writing assessments that encourage formula approaches often squeeze creativity out of young authors. (For an excellent examination of the impact of state writing assessments on student writing, see George Hillocks' (2002) *The Testing Trap*.)

What is creativity in writing? It's hard to find a definition everyone can agree upon, but typically it is associated with innovation, invention, productivity, authorship, imagination, originality, and expressiveness.

How do you recognize creativity in writing, and how do you encourage it? Creativity is a fresh approach. It's trying something new, like creating a tale of a boy wizard-in-training at a school for wizardry surrounded by fascinating characters, like J. K. Rowling did in the Harry Potter series. It's adopting a different point of view, like John Sciesczka (1989) did when he re-wrote the classic three little pigs story, but told it from the viewpoint of the wolf in *The True Story of the Three Little Pigs*. It's re-doing something old in a fresh way, like Bill Martin Jr. and Stephen Kellogg (1998) did when they re-told the "dark, dark wood" tale in *A Beasty Story*, adding new characters and a subplot and a surprise ending to the old story.

In your writing workshop, you'll see creativity when your students try something new or when they take a chance or when they imitate something they have read and make it their own. There's probably no way to teach creativity, but there are many ways to encourage it and to set up a writing workshop atmosphere where students will feel free to take creative chances. Here are some ways to teach for creativity:

1. Creatives are stimulated by other creatives. When you read an author whose creative approach impresses you, mention that to your young students. The concept of creativity will be abstract to students. But when you read *The True Story of the Three Little Pigs* (Sciesczka, 1989) and note that the author took a creative approach in telling this story from the viewpoint of the wolf, that he tried a perspective that had never been tried before, students begin to see exactly what creativity means. Will they then begin to take familiar stories and write them from the viewpoint of different characters ad nauseum? Perhaps. But this just gives them experience in a creative approach to writing—even if it were not their idea originally. It makes no difference; the more they "think out of the box" when they write, the more comfortable they will be with these types of approaches.

2. Take a chance yourself in the writing you share with students and in the modeled writing you do in front of them. Creativity almost always involves taking a risk. The fact that you have modeled risk-taking makes it much more likely your young writers will follow your example.

3. Realize that when young writers take a chance with something new, sometimes other areas of their writing suffer because they have put so much creative energy into the piece at hand. A creative approach will often be deficient in grammar or spelling or punctuation. Honor the creative approach, and later remind the young writer that the writing is so good that it really deserves a good job of editing so the mistakes won't distract readers.

4. Creativity typically follows fluency. The occasional cook doesn't create a creative soufflé. Creative chefs are those who spend hours in the kitchen, trying different combinations and cooking for people who comment on the dishes they serve. The more students write—in an atmosphere that shows examples of creativity and gives them the freedom to take risks—the more they will attempt the type of divergent approaches we typically call creative.

In Your Writer's Notebook . . .

Write about whether you consider yourself creative as a writer. In what other areas of your life do you exhibit creativity? How have you developed creativity in those areas? Why (or why not) do you exhibit creativity in your writing?

Who's the most creative (in any area) person you know? Use the show, don't tell principle to describe that person.

In your classroom writer's workshop . . .

Let your class use the dictionary and the Internet to define creativity. Then, apply that definition to writing. Then, let them come up with some books they consider creative. (You might share the ones mentioned in today's workshop to "prime the pump.") Make a Creative Writing chart that includes author, title, and what's creative in that book. Let students add to that list as they encounter other books and stories during the year. You will probably find them consulting that chart to come up with creative approaches in their own writing.

Writeaerobics Workout #31

Flashbacks: Adding
the Perspective of Time

> You won't, in general, insert a flashback right in the middle of fascinating action. That merely frustrates the reader, who is trying to find out what happens next—not what happened a long time ago.
>
> But at a certain moment he will want a flashback. He'll want to know how things got like this, what makes these people the way they are.
>
> *Jonathan Penner*

Flashbacks are a literary device you should definitely add to your bag of author's tricks. And then . . . show your young writers how they can use flashbacks, too.

Flashbacks go back in time into a character's past and explore events that help readers understand what's going on in the present. In fact, the simplest definition of a flashback is that it is any scene that happened before the present story began. The best flashbacks are short and illuminate the present story in an important way. Let's say you're writing about a child who frequently gets angry with his teacher at school for no apparent reason. You write about an outburst, using the show, don't tell technique to involve the reader, then you flash back to that child several years ago, when he was told that his family had been killed in an automobile accident.

If you need a good example of flashback, re-read Ambrose Bierce's (1970) short story "An Occurrence at Owl Creek Bridge." The story starts with a noose around a man's neck. He falls, and—while he is in the air—reviews his life and sees an escape. Then the rope jerks tight and breaks his neck. The story itself takes about 30 seconds, but the flashback extends over several pages. "Occurrence at Owl Creek Bridge" breaks the "rule" about flashbacks being short, but it illustrates their power.

Why do writers use flashbacks? Because they want to involve you first in the story, to get you engrossed in the problem and to make you care about the characters. Then, having hooked you, they digress to a flashback to deliver essential information that will help you better understand the characters.

How do you know you need a flashback? Is there some information from a character's past that would help readers—if they knew that information—care more about the story itself? Or maybe better understand why the character is doing what he's doing?

How do writers move into flashbacks? It can be really simple, as in the technique Jon Scieszka (1991) used in his *Knights of the Kitchen Table*. The story begins with three obviously modern-day kids accosted in a medieval forest by a Black Knight, who eventually begins to charge toward them on his horse, his lance threatening their imminent demise. That's chapter 1. Scieszka begins chapter 2 with the simplest of flashback devices:

> But before the Black Knight arrives, maybe I should explain how three regular guys happened to find themselves facing death by shish-kebab.
>
> It all started with my birthday party. My two best friends, Fred and Sam, were over at my house. (p. 7)

You'll find a much more sophisticated flashback in Patricia MacLachlan's (1985) Newbery-winning classic *Sarah, Plain and Tall*. At the beginning of the book, Anna is talking to her brother Caleb about the day he was born. After sharing that familiar story again with Caleb, Anna becomes lost in thought remembering her mother. Watch the subtle turn that introduces the flashback:

> I wiped my hands on my apron and went to the window. Outside the prairie reaches out and touched the places where the sky came down. Though winter was nearly over, there were patches of snow and ice everywhere. I looked at the long dirt road that crawled across the plains, remembering the morning that Mama had died, cruel and sunny. They had come for her in a wagon and taken her away to be buried. (p. 5)

Flashbacks are difficult to write. Once a young writer asked Sinclair Lewis how best to handle them in fiction. Lewis' answer: "Don't."

But that assumes we can only use literary devices we can handle deftly, with accomplishment. That takes too much of the fun out of writing. So don't be afraid to let your young writers play with flashback, especially after they have learned to identify it in the books they enjoy.

In Your Writer's Notebook . . .

Think about a conflict you have had with someone close to you, perhaps an argument with a spouse or a friend. Try to pick an argument where you were offended because of something about which you were quite sensitive—because of something that happened to you years ago. (Example: Let's say you play first base on the school's faculty softball team, and you let an easy grounder go right through your glove. Everyone laughs and kids you about it, and you smile on the outside but it hurts you deeply. Not because of the blown ground ball, but because when you were a child you had struck out in an important game and your teammates said they had lost because of you. Their ridicule crushed you. And now, your friends' innocent joking brings all that childhood anguish back. Or: Maybe someone tries to give you harmless advice and you blow up—not because of what that person said, but because your mother never accepted you and was constantly correcting you.) Get the idea? Begin with your present-day story, then flash back to the "story behind the story."

In Your Classroom Writer's Workshop . . .

Put together a craft lesson on flashback. Look for examples in stories your children enjoy. But not just in books: Movies and TV shows offer great illustrations of the use of flashback. Sometimes a video clip can be the best illustration. If you show a clip, you might first examine how the filmmaker did the flashback, and then write just that part as a class activity, approaching it as a story, not a TV show or movie.

Start a list of flashbacks in stories, listing the story and the nature of the flashback. Pay special attention to how the author introduced the flashback. What words were used to move into the flashback? And how did the author transition out of the flashback into the main story?

Bring a short story you wrote about something in your life. Make copies so each of your writers can have one. Then, just tell the "story behind the story," the story that would explain your actions. With your class, write the flashback into the story you distributed.

Writeaerobics Workout #32

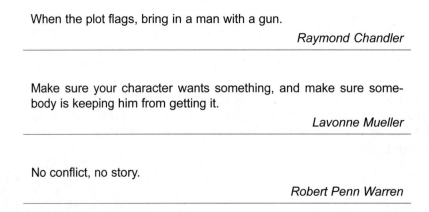

Throwing Obstacles at Your Characters

> When the plot flags, bring in a man with a gun.
>
> *Raymond Chandler*

> Make sure your character wants something, and make sure somebody is keeping him from getting it.
>
> *Lavonne Mueller*

> No conflict, no story.
>
> *Robert Penn Warren*

Let's say this is the plot outline for Martin and Archambault's (1985) classic tale *The Ghost-Eye Tree*: One night, mother told a little boy and his sister to go to the dairy for some milk. So they went to the farm of Mr. Cowlander, the dairyman, and returned with the milk, which they gave to their mother.

Boring. A story no young reader would care about. Actually, the summary above is the basic outline of this story. But we've left out one crucial element: the problem. On the way to Mr. Cowlander's the children had to walk past the ghost-eye tree, which they believed to be haunted. What happened when they encountered the "problem" of ghost-eye is the heart of the story.

In fact, it's what turns a narrative into a story. A narrative is just a chronological recounting of events. If you were to tell about your day, you'd probably have a narrative. You'd describe getting up, making breakfast, helping your family get off to work or school, teaching your class, and so forth. That's a narrative. But if, on the way to school, you were involved in a six-car pileup and were treated by paramedics, your narrative has just turned into a story. A story is a narrative with a problem, a conflict, an obstacle thrown in the path of the characters.

Problems add tension to a plot. Skillful writers build tension, release it, and then build it again. In *The Ghost-Eye Tree* (Martin & Archambault, 1985), for example, the children nervously walk past the tree on the way to Mr. Cowlander's. Nothing happens—no ghostly manifestations. The little boy and his sister celebrate, singing "There's no such thing as a ghost." But after they got their milk, they had to walk back past the tree. Martin and Archambault set up the problem once again—and this time they do encounter the "ghost."

Authors have all sorts of ways to present problems their characters must face and work through.

- If the character must be somewhere at a specific time, he can be late or miss the appointment altogether.
- If the character needs to be alone, he can be surrounded by people. If he needs someone to be with him for support or comfort or protection, he can be alone.
- If the character needs to find something, the search can be difficult or fruit-less.
- If the character needs to communicate with someone, the note can be destroyed or misinterpreted, or the computer is down so that the e-mail cannot go through, or the telephone lines are tied up so the call cannot be completed.
- If the character needs to succeed at the audition to get a place on the cheerleading squad, a broken ankle can make the tryout impossible.

A good way to create problems is to think about the character's goals—what she wants out of life or what she wants to happen in a certain situation. You can do this by answering the following questions:

- Who or what could keep her from achieving her goals?
- Where could things go wrong?
- When would be the worst time for something to go wrong?
- How could things go wrong? List a sequence of events that would present the problem.

In more sophisticated stories, characters will not encounter just one obstacle. Characters go from one problem to the other until they finally succeed—or fail—at their goal.

Helping students to see how stories really work by analyzing the types of problems authors devise for their characters can give young writers ideas about the types of problems they can present to the characters in their stories. Even young writers can differentiate narratives from stories and begin to see what types of obstacles characters encounter. As they grow more sophisticated as readers, this sophistication inevitably works its way into their writing.

In Your Writer's Notebook . . .

In the back of your writer's notebook, write down "Problems" as a page heading. Start keeping a list of problems/obstacles/conflicts that characters can encounter. This may be from your own reading, from TV or movies, or just things you see happening in your own life.

Also, list as many problems from your own life as you can remember. It may range from always being the last one chosen for any team in elementary school, to the death of a parent or close friend, to finding a snake in your back yard, to facing the failure of a marriage. Pick one to write about. Write about how you faced and overcame—or were defeated by—that obstacle.

In Your Classroom Writer's Workshop . . .

Start a class chart on problems and conflicts faced by characters in books your students read. You can make the chart as sophisticated as you want. Some columns for the chart might include: title of the book, author, name of character, setting, type of problem, resolution, and so forth. Your young writers might also want to do charts for TV shows and movies. The object of this exercise is to help them see types of obstacles writers throw at characters. This will also serve as a resource for their writing, as your students begin to use variations of those same types of problems in their own pieces.

Writeaerobics Workout #33

Teaching Grammar

> Teachers do not have to abandon grammar, but if the chief goal is writing improvement and not grammar for its own sake, grammar instruction will have to be much more selective and much more cost-efficient than in the past.
>
> *Rei R. Noguchi*

Chances are, your students' view of grammar is so warped that you'll need to start all over again in helping them to understand grammar and its purpose. Grammar has been taught to them as decontextualized facts and rules. So now, they see it as another hoop to jump through in school—memorize the information and regurgitate it correctly for the teacher.

We want to move students to see grammar like carpenters see nails. For carpenters, nails are tools you use to hold boards together. Carpenters don't celebrate nails or talk about nails or study nails; they use them to build things. True, carpenters know a lot about nails. People who don't build things see all nails as pretty much equal—they're made out of metal and they have one pointy end to drive into wood and a head to hit with a hammer. But carpenters know nails come in all kinds of sizes and weights and functions—some to drive into concrete, some for wood, some for sheet rock, and so forth.

If you apprenticed yourself as a novice to a master carpenter, he would not begin by teaching you about the types and functions of nails. Instead, you would begin by learning to build things, and in the context of building, he would teach you about the different kinds of nails you would use.

Writers teach grammar like carpenters teach nails. Students write every day, and in the context of writing learn more about the "tools" writers use—the various grammatical elements and constructions.

Jeffrey Wilhelm (2001) explained it this way:

> A decade of research in cognitive science demonstrates that how something is taught and the situation in which it is taught are part and parcel of what is learned. The contention that all cognition is "situated" means that teaching formal grammar through worksheets and sentence

diagramming results in kids who are good at (you guessed it!) doing worksheets and diagramming sentences. If we want students to use language more correctly in their own writing and speaking, then we must teach them to do so in that meaning-producing situation that will co-produce and support that learning. What we need is the contextualized learning of correct language use.

To teach language use correctly, the context I suggest is that of the students' own writing. . . .

When I told my seventh graders to put their grammar books into the cabinet and explained why (because we would be learning how to use language in the context of really using it in meaningful activities), they cheered. They knew what we should know; we learn what we actually have the opportunity to practice and do in the real world. (p. 62)

One writing teacher, when he teaches grammar, always uses the phrase "Writers use . . ." If you walk into his writing workshop, you might find him talking about adverbs, adjectives, proper nouns, or active and passive voices of verbs. But as you listen to him talk about these grammatical elements, you'll also hear him say "Writers use the active voice to . . ." , "Writers use adjectives to. . .", "Writers use specific proper nouns to . . ." He never wants his students to divorce nails from carpentry, or the use of the parts (grammar) as building blocks of the whole (good writing).

In Your Writer's Notebook . . .

You will be successful as a grammar teacher to the extent that you begin to think of grammatical principles as the building blocks of good writing, not as precepts to be learned because the curriculum demands it. One of the best ways to re-orient your thinking is to begin to see how good writing uses those grammatical principles (though most professional writers do this by "feel"—from extensive reading—rather than by design).

So try this: Find a paragraph you like in a book you are reading and analyze the grammar. Do what you remember doing from school—underline subjects, double underline verbs, circle adjectives, box adverbs, and so forth. Note whether the verbs are active or passive. Note clauses and their placement in the sentences.

Then, in your writer's notebook, make a statement—maybe only one sentence—that summarizes some grammatical principle you have noticed. Maybe it will be that the writer begins lots of sentences with adverb clauses, and this delays the subject so far into the sentence that it makes the paragraph hard to read. Maybe it's simply that the writer has written a long paragraph without the use of a single adverb, but the verbs are so strong that they don't need modifying. Maybe you notice that the writer has written the entire paragraph in the passive voice, perhaps because he wanted to slow down the flow and let the reader linger over this paragraph of description.

Don't worry if this exercise doesn't seem to benefit you a lot. Try it again several times, perhaps with a different author and different book. You will begin to see how the grammatical parts work together for the writer. When you get really comfortable with this activity, pick a paragraph from a book your students enjoy and try it as a class activity.

In Your Classroom Writer's Workshop . . .

A fun exercise to kick-start writing workshops and to teach grammar at the same time is to write "fumblerules." These are mistakes that call attention to the rules themselves. Here are some illustrations to get you started:

- Avoid commas, that are not necessary.
- Verbs has to agree with their subjects.
- Don't use no double negatives.
- Writing carefully, dangling participles should not be used.
- Don't verb nouns.

Writeaerobics Workout #34

Writing as a Verbal Activity

> Have you ever cradled a pile of playing cards after a game and found yourself holding a misaligned deck, with cards angling out in all directions? Then you began to shake and bounce and massage cards, and almost automatically they reconstitute themselves into the familiar cubelike pack.
>
> Talking can have a similar effect on the ideas floating around in your imagination.
>
> *Carl Sessions Stepp*

Two things happen during composition. The first is conceptualization. That's when you think about what you plan to write about. If you are writing about something that happened to you, for instance, you picture that event in your mind. You try to write what you're seeing in your mind's eye.

We move from conceptualization to writing. That's actually getting the ideas and images and stories and concepts and information into written form. And many times, that's where the frustration comes in. We know what we want to say; it's just that we have trouble getting it into words. In other words, we're having difficulty moving from the conceptualization stage to the writing stage.

And the younger you are, the bigger the leap between the two. In school, we take the normal conceptualization/writing gap and add (for younger children) problems with the physical act of writing, or fear of grading, or just the fact that your brain moves so much faster than your hand.

Many writers have discovered a tool that is too seldom used in school: the intermediate step of verbalization. In other words, "talking out" what we plan to write about.

Frequently, when you speak, you hear yourself express ideas, insights, and connections you never even knew you had. Free from the burden of handwriting your ideas or typing them, you let them flow with more fluency.

Writing coaches know this principle is perhaps the most powerful concept behind the writing conference. (For more details on conferencing, see *Writer to Writer: How to Conference Young Authors* (Thomason, 1998).) When we engage writers in talking about what they have written, we help them think through the process. We ask questions that reflect what real readers would want to know, and in the process give young writers the opportunity to verbalize that information and tell those stories and supply the needed background and detail. In other words, they are verbalizing the information that needs to be in their stories. Then they can write down what they just heard themselves say.

Imagine two teachers approaching a writer in workshop who has just written about her excitement when she passed her brown belt test in tae kwon do. One teacher says, "Why don't you add more details that explain how you felt?"

The other says: "Teresa, I wish I could have seen you when your instructor tied that belt around your waist. Do you think that's the most difficult challenge you've ever faced in your life? (Response.) Would you do it all over again if you had to start now on the white belt level? (Response.) Can you picture your tae kwon do school when you were awarded the belt? Do you remember what your instructor said to you as he tied the belt around you? Do you remember what you were thinking right then?"

Those are simple questions, but they are designed to get the writer to think back to the time her belt was awarded. The first teacher made an assessment, followed by an assignment. When she left, the student had the task of following the teacher's directive.

But the second teacher involved the young writer in conversation. Those were not just idle questions. They were designed to get the writer to think back to the night of the awarding of the belt, to picture it in her mind, to recall her thinking, and to make some value judgments about the way tae kwon do has benefited her.

The second teacher elicited verbalization from the young writer in all those areas. There they were—all those words just hanging out there in the air, ripe for writing down and using in her piece.

Talking works well with another person or a small group, and it also works when you're by yourself. One writer tells of just chattering away to herself every morning as she commutes to her job, "talking out" her story lines, developing her characters, describing scenes, and the like. She doesn't write until late at night, but she prewrites every day in the car, just opening her mouth and letting the stream of consciousness flow. If the idea is really good or the image especially vivid, she turns on her microcassette tape recorder and records as much as she can. That night, before she writes, she plays back her recordings. Talk about pre-writing! Sometimes all she does is copy down what she said orally in the car, edit for style, and polish.

So whether you have the sympathetic ear of a listener or a hand-held tape recorder, talk out your writing whenever you can. Verbalization always makes the writing easier.

For Your Writer's Notebook . . .

Write a childhood memory in your writer's notebook. Try to pick something you think your class would enjoy hearing about. Then wait a few days (so you can forget some of the details of how you wrote the story) and tell the same story to your class.

Then write the story, or a portion of the story, as a modeled writing or a shared writing. Read both versions—the one you did at home and the one you did in class following the oral telling—to your young writers.

For Your Classroom Writer's Workshop . . .

Let your students do the same activity, but in groups. Have them identify a story they would like to write and then tell that story to someone else or to a small group. Show the group how to respond to a story by asking questions about areas they would like to know more about. After they have shared the story orally, your writers can put it on paper. When students discover the value of "talking out" a story or an opinion (for a persuasive piece) or instructions (for a how-to-do-it piece), they have discovered one of the most valuable pre-writing exercises.

How People Learn to Write: Implications for Instruction

> *I hear and I forget.*
>
> *I see and I remember.*
>
> *I do and I understand.*
>
> Chinese proverb

The art of teaching is the art of assisting discovery.

Mark Van Doren

It's the most basic question for any writing teacher: How do people learn to write?

Many teachers resent any mention of "theory." They consider the ultimate put-down of an inservice presentation to be a charge that the speaker presented "too much theory." But theory is a statement of principles from which we derive a practice. Every parent, for instance, has a theory about how children should be taught and disciplined. Some believe in corporal punishment; others avoid it at all costs. Every parent wants a well-behaved child. But well-meaning parents who desire the same outcomes—because of their theories about childrearing—approach correction in radically different ways. Their theories on discipline give rise to their practice in actually dealing with their children.

Every teacher has theories on how people learn to write—and those theories are the basis of classroom practice. Nobody stated it better than Brian Cambourne (1988):

> What teachers actually do when engaged in the act of teaching is motivated by what they believe about learners and what they believe about the processes which underlie learning. Like most human activity, teaching behavior is not a random sequence of haphazard events. Teachers plan the lessons they give, buy the materials they use, allocate the time they have, say the things they say, treat children the way they do, evaluate the way they evaluate, reward and punish the way they do, and so on, because of what they believe about the way learning occurs and how it can be brought about. I regard this set of beliefs

about learning as a "theory" or a "model" which each teacher carries around inside her head. (p. 17)

This book is based on several important theoretical constructs—beliefs the author has about how people learn to write. Here are some of the ideas about writing upon which this book is based:

- You learn to write by writing, not by studying about writing.

- Writing teachers should be writers, and they should model a literate lifestyle.

- Literature should be appreciated as literature, but it should also be used as a writing model.

- Skills (like grammar and punctuation) should be taught in the context of writing.

- Writing teachers should teach the process, and the best way to do that is to demonstrate writing through modeled writing in class.

- A workshop atmosphere makes for the most effective writing instruction. That workshop should include writing talk, one-on-one conversations about writing while it's in process.

- Students will only take ownership of their writing if they are allowed to choose their own topics.

- Publication is necessary to make writing authentic.

To the author of this book, these statements represent absolute truths about writing. Therefore, they form the basis of a writing pedagogy. What we do in a writing classroom, as Cambourne said, is always based on what we believe.

In Your Writer's Notebook . . .

Assume you were writing a letter to parents—or perhaps even to your young writers—about what you believe about how people learn to write. Write that letter in your writer's notebook. Be sure that your "theory" actually translates into your classroom pedagogy.

In Your Classroom Writer's Workshop . . .

Our students should understand our theories about learning to write. One of the best ways to help them see how people learn to write is to let them brainstorm ways in which people learn a skill. You might pick playing basketball or cooking or learning to dance or to paint. Tell your class you want them to list ways a teacher would help someone become, say, a dancer or a painter. Tell them to begin from the beginning. When they brainstorm the teaching of these skills, you will find that almost everything they list has an exact parallel in teaching writing, if you are doing it well. For instance, a dance teacher will demonstrate a step to a student and then let the student try it out with the teacher watching and "talking her through" the step. In the writing classroom, that's modeled writing and conferencing. Your students will benefit from seeing why you do what you do in writing workshop.

Your Approach to Writing: Everyone's Different . . . Live With It

I don't write a word of the article until I have the end.

Nora Ephron

The most important sentence in any article is the first one.

William Zinsser

With novels it's the first line that's important.

Elie Wiesel

I always write the end of everything first.

Truman Capote

Listening to other writers talk about their craft can be inspiring, but it can also be dangerous. Especially if the writer is successful, we tend to think his or her approach is "the right way." There's no such thing. This can be confusing for young writers and even for older writers who are looking for the "one best approach" to the craft. So one successful writer says he never begins a story until he knows how it will end; another says he sets up characters and lets the story happen in front of him as he writes. One writer says she never moves on until she has perfected what she has already written; another says she never even looks at what she has written until she finishes the book or article. One writer outlines before beginning; another has never written an outline at any stage of the writing process. If you look at any book of quotes on writing by well-known authors, you can find ample support for widely divergent approaches to writing.

Young authors want to know whose approach is right.

Too bad. That comes partly from the way we have taught writing, especially when we say that a certain approach is the way it's done. Typically the approach is presented in brightly colored graphic organizers on the wall, boxes connected to other boxes by arrows. A flow chart for writing.

Problem is, the chart doesn't work. As a generality, it does present various elements of writing in an order many people find helpful. But consider this: We call that the writing process, as if there is only one.

There are all kinds of pre-writing strategies, and we have taught that pre-writing typically consists of brainstorming or outlining or completing a Venn diagram—something a teacher can see evidence of in the classroom. But consider the writer who was standing in a hallway, looking out a window when he was approached by a friend.

"What are you doing?" the writer's friend asked.

"Writing," he replied.

The writer's friend walked away with a puzzled look.

And indeed he was writing. It was his style, before he ever sat down to write, to mentally review the story line. Though he wasn't doing anything we might identify with writing, he was preparing to write in his mind.

Once you are committed to writing as a way of life and know you will be writing something every day—or at least almost every day—your entire life becomes a brainstorming session for writing. When you are driving or cooking or taking a shower or perhaps teaching a lesson on the life cycle of the caterpillar, some part of your mind is processing what you will be writing about. Prewriting isn't necessarily a pen-and-paper exercise so much as a lifestyle and a way of thinking.

If you love military history and you tour Europe, you will constantly be looking for the next battlefield or museum. You will look for and see points of military importance that totally escape others you might be traveling with. But let's say you could care less about generals and battles; instead, you appreciate gourmet cooking. Now your tour of Europe will be completely different. You won't even notice the signs pointing to major battlefields or the statues commemorating the victors. Instead, you will be thinking about the five-star restaurant where you'll dine this evening. The historian and the gourmet might well travel together, but they will experience different realities. The writer, committed to writing as a lifestyle, sifts through his day looking for characters and stories and illustrations and textures to weave into his writing. Maybe the "writing process" you teach in class isn't the one you follow yourself. Don't be concerned; there is no one right way to approach writing. In fact, the only major thing writers have in common is that they all write.

And as you teach, remember that your students have different personalities, learning styles, and writing habits. Outlining and completing Venn diagrams fit the writing styles of many students. For others, though, prewriting may well be talking with a friend about the writing task at hand or even staring off into space.

In Your Writer's Notebook . . .

Write about your writing process, how you write. Where do you prefer to write? When? How do you get started? What's your favorite method of prewriting—or do you instead just begin to write and see what happens on paper?

In Your Classroom Writer's Workshop . . .

Conduct a discussion of "writing styles" with your class. Read what you wrote in your writer's notebook about your own style. Students should see that you will teach them many prewriting "tricks," but those serve the same purpose kitchen implements serve. You don't use a spatula on everything. It's just one implement among many you have at your disposal.

Writeaerobics Workout #37

To Prompt
or Not to Prompt

> In second and third grade they told us to write things that we have not done or even know for god sake.
>
> *A fourth grader, commenting on prompt-driven writing*

Constructivists claim that prompts make young writers dependent on the ideas of others and destroy authenticity. Skills-oriented teachers say that prompts prepare children for the rest of their education (characterized by writing topics supplied by teachers and professors) and for the real world of work, where people frequently write about topics not of their own choosing. Test-preparation manuals claim that prompts prepare students for state writing achievement tests.

Who's right? All of them. And none of them. It's like asking if water is good for you. Of course it is, and you should drink at least eight glasses a day. If you don't get it, you'll die. But if that's the sum total of your intake, you'll also die. Your diet must be balanced among a number of different ingredients.

And so should your writing diet.

Many writers point to the necessity of learning to choose your own topic, of not being tied to someone else's writing agenda. Writing workshops come alive when students can write about what they know about, what's important to them. This teaches them to begin with an idea and develop it, making all the choices writers have to make about genre and style. Maybe the writer scored the winning run in a Little League game the night before. He might want to write about why he loves baseball or to tell the story of the game. He might want to draw on his baseball expertise to make up a story about a kid who comes to bat with the bases loaded in the bottom of the ninth inning in the championship game, a modern-day *Casey at the Bat*. He may write poetry about how spring wouldn't be spring without baseball, or expository prose about how baseball is a superior game to football or hockey. These choices turn writer's workshop into a real workshop—just like an artists' workshop, where choices about medium and color and texture are commonplace. Writers who make these choices are more invested in what they write, and they write because they already know or because they want to know. Either way, the pieces are more interesting and have the potential of showing real voice.

The best way to teach topic choice is to model it. You should spend part of your writing workshop writing yourself on most days. Many workshops begin with a Status of the Class meeting, where young writers share briefly what they will be writing about that day. Teachers should share during this time, too. Let your students see you developing topics, just like they do. And tell them why you chose to write about a certain topic. It's the most valuable lesson on the mechanics of topic choice you'll ever teach.

So should you avoid prompts? Certainly not. Give them occasional writing assignments to help them stretch their writing muscles. This gets students out of their writing ruts and helps them take chances with new skills. After you have taught a craft lesson on dialogue, you might ask them to write about a conversation between two characters, telling the story purely in dialogue. When you introduce any new skill, you might ask writers to apply that in a piece they write that day. If you make up prompts, keep them as open-ended as possible. Instead of asking "What would you do with a pot of gold you found at the end of a rainbow?", phrase it like this: "Tell what you might find at the end of a rainbow." For a great source on all kinds of creative writing ideas, see Marjorie Frank's (1995) *If You're Trying to Teach Kids How to Write . . . You've Gotta Have This Book*. For adults who need to kick-start their muse, the best book hands-down is *Writing Without the Muse: 60 Beginning Exercises for the Creative Writer* by Beth Joselow (1995), which has literally hundreds of writing ideas. When you finish that book, or even a small portion of it, you should be well on your way to being a comfortable writer with lots of ideas of your own.

Do prompts help prepare students for state writing achievement tests? Again, the answer isn't as simple as yes or no. Perhaps the best answer is that they are far overrated as test-preparation tools. It would seem to be logical that if students are going to be writing to a prompt on the test, we should give them lots of prompts to prepare them for what they will actually be doing on test day. And that's true, to a limited extent. Students should certainly write to sample prompts of the type they may face. They should write with the same time constraints they will face on the test. It is even valuable to give students a lot of sample prompts and share with them how prompts are written. Then let them write their own prompts. You can take their prompts and discuss how a writer would address these prompts if they actually appeared on the test. But all too often, a whole year of writing instruction is wasted in writing to prompts. Students burn out on writing and turn against the process, because they can't separate test-writing from real writing.

The good news is that students who have written regularly and developed fluency in writing by choosing and developing their own topics actually do a better job of writing to state prompts. Teach test-writing as a separate genre of writing. Several months before the test, talk about the test format and how prompts are constructed. Share a lot of prompts and talk about how you might respond to these prompts. Have the class write their own prompts and choose their favorite. Then you write a modeled writing to that prompt. In other words, pretend this student-generated prompt is the writing topic you have to address on a test. Then just write out loud. Let students watch as you think aloud about your choices as a writer and how you will address the prompt. Let them watch as you write your piece, doing exactly what they will have to do on the test.

As test day approaches, increase the frequency of prompts. But remember, your students' success will not come because you have drilled them on prompts. It will come because you have helped them to think like writers and to develop writing fluency.

In Your Writer's Notebook . . .

The first writing idea presented in *Writing Without the Muse* (Joselow, 1995) is to create a portrait of a person who has been important to you. Joselow suggests that you begin by making notes on the following five questions:

1. Write down the first five characteristics that come to mind when you think of this person.

2. Explain the prominence of each of these characteristics: Why does it stand out?

3. How have you been influenced by this person?

4. What have you missed in this relationship—what would you like to make different in it?

5. Briefly outline a story about this person that seems to reveal his/her character at its: best, worst, most surprising, most typical. (pp. 17–18)

The goal of a book like this is not to make you dependent on having a topic spoon-fed to you whenever you write. It's to let you in on the thinking process of writers—to see what writers write about. The more you write, the more ideas you will get. If you follow Joselow's ideas above, for instance, you'll probably come up with a lot of different pieces you could write about this person who has been so important in your life.

In Your Classroom Writer's Workshop . . .

Most states publish a collection of student writing reflecting the various score points on the test. For instance, if the lowest grade is 1 and the highest is 6, you should have access to typical papers at each score point from 1 to 6. Share these with your writers during workshop. Help them to assess the papers, looking for strengths and weaknesses. This will help to familiarize them with successful ways to approach prompts.

Vocabulary and the Writer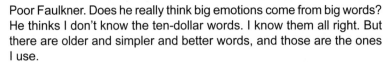

> Poor Faulkner. Does he really think big emotions come from big words?
> He thinks I don't know the ten-dollar words. I know them all right. But
> there are older and simpler and better words, and those are the ones
> I use.
>
> *Ernest Hemingway*

Too much vocabulary instruction has obviously been designed by non-writers.

Much vocabulary instruction consists of introducing young writers to new words out of context. They are listed, defined, and used in sentences. Students frequently have to learn to spell them and use them meaningfully in sentences. Sometimes, they are sent on word scavenger hunts to find examples of the words in some particular unit.

No bigger waste of time exists in the classroom.

Let's begin at the beginning: The purpose of vocabulary instruction should be to increase the arsenal of words available for young writers. We should study vocabulary so that we have a wider and richer array of choices when we write and when we speak.

And why do we need a rich array of word choices? So we can make writing come alive. So that we can use just the write word to describe the right person or action or object. Vocabulary is to a writer as the skill of bunting is to a baseball player. Little Leaguers learn to bunt because there are certain situations in a baseball game when the object is not to get a hit, but to move the runner along to the next base and therefore into scoring position. For the batter, a bunt is typically an automatic out. But it's a skill serious baseball players realize they need to be successful. So while they might love the home run swing more, batters spend hours working on their skill at bunting, so they will have that skill when the right situation comes along.

Writers collect words for the same reason. Some teachers post lists of words on their walls and label them "exciting words." But there's no such thing. A word is just a collection of letters. A word cannot be exciting or dull. Big words are not better than small ones. Writers love words that help them express an idea with precision, words that put pictures in the minds of readers.

No writer ever said he or she developed a good vocabulary from studying de-contextualized vocabulary lists. Writers don't even talk about vocabulary—that's only a school concept. Ever hear someone say Pat Conroy or John Grisham or J. K. Rowling has a great vocabulary? They do, of course. And they use the words they have collected through reading and listening to paint scenes we remember in their books.

Because they write every day, they are constantly on the lookout for words that will communicate their concepts, much like a gardener is constantly on the lookout for new plants and a carpenter for useful tools. Too much vocabulary instruction begins with the premise that we need to increase students' vocabularies so they will be able to write effectively and enjoy writing more. But that's backward. Instead, we need to help students write effectively and enjoy writing more so they will see words like writers do—as tools to communicate more effectively in prose and poetry.

Many writers do their own vocabulary study from the books they read. When they find a unique word or a turn of phrase they like, they write it down in their writer's notebook. And sometimes, that's as far as it goes. But like gardeners turning compost, sometimes they return to that phrase and play with it, using it in their own sentence or adapting it to something they are working on. Writers collect words and images and phrases, hoarding them away until they can find ways to use them in their own work.

In Your Writer's Notebook . . .

Set aside some pages in your writer's notebook for words and phrases you lifted from other authors. It could be just a word you like the sound of. Or maybe a phrase from a poem or a novel. If it's longer, put the name of the book, the author (and any other bibliographical information you would like to keep), and the page number. You might come up with categories like great verbs or descriptions of people or descriptions of places. If the passage is too long to copy, just put the book and the page number. These lists will come in handy for you as you write and as you come up with your own craft lessons.

In Your Classroom Writer's Workshop . . .

A key to good vocabulary is the use of specific nouns (not "dog," but "a prissy white French poodle named Fifi"). Get a copy of Carolyn Lesser's (1997) *Storm in the Desert*. The book's description of desert life is a perfect object lesson of effective word choice in vocabulary used to paint word pictures. Take any page of the book and substitute weaker verbs for Lesser's strong verbs and more generic nouns for Lesser's specific nouns. Show your class what a difference effective word choice makes in good writing.

Writeaerobics Workout #39

Writing Simply

> Try to write like you're having a conversation with your best friend.
>
> *Phil LaVelle*

> Clarity is crucial to good writing of any kind. Whether the communication is a news story, press release, letter, memo or report, its merit rests on its understandability. If it's unclear, it can only bewilder, annoy or mislead.
>
> *Paula LaRocque*

One of the ways that non-writers have co-opted writing instruction is by pushing the idea that complicated is better than simple, long is better than short, and wordy is better than terse. In short, they write to impress, not to express. But they only impress other non-writers. Writers are never impressed by needless complexity.

Typically, muddy or pretentious prose hides sloppy or careless thinking. Non-writers will sometimes even say, "You're over-simplifying" or "You're dumbing down that idea." Actually, the best communicators have usually been the clearest communicators. Think of the straightforward prose of Ernest Hemingway or F. Scott Fitzgerald or Winston Churchill or Joan Didion or even Abraham Lincoln. President Lincoln spoke only two minutes at Gettysburg; the main orator, Edward Everett, spoke almost two hours. Everyone remembers the lean prose of the Gettysburg Address, but who remembers Everett or what he said?

Good writing avoids long, uncommon words, sentences and paragraphs that go on forever, and constructions that hide meaning rather than expose it. In fact, that type of writing is probably copied from bureaucrats who wanted to hide behind language rather that use it to communicate. So they talked about collateral damage rather than casualties, revenue enhancement rather than tax increases, ongoing highway maintenance programs rather than roadwork, and technical adjustments rather than market drops.

A physics professor at New York University, Alan D. Sokal, once showed that pretentious language can hide the sloppiest of thinking. He wrote an article, published as serious scholarship in an academic journal, in which he said, among other things, that scientific discourse "for all its undeniable value, cannot assert a privileged epistemological status with respect to counter-hegemonic narratives emanating from dissident or marginalized communities" (quoted in Patricia O'Connor, 1999, p. 55). The thesis of his long-winded article? There's no real world; we made it up. No one caught onto the fact that Skokal had perpetrated a hoax on the academic community, a gag, until he confessed.

In the past, many of the non-writers who taught writing honored big words and long sentences and pompous prose. And even now, people who studied writing in those classes find it difficult just to say what they mean in simple language. Too many are victims of what writing coach Paula LaRocque (2002) calls the Diamond Jim Brady theory of communication. Brady, an American financier in the 1800s, became a millionaire by selling for a railroad supply company and investing his profits. Diamond Jim became known for his tasteless display of jewelry. When asked why he wore so many gaudy gems, he is said to have replied, "Them as has 'em wears 'em." LaRocque calls this "the paradox of good taste":

> Good taste shows restraint and simplicity: Them as has 'em wears just one or two—but the *right* one or two. The rest stay in the safe for another occasion. It's the same with words. Owning many words informs and enriches our communication even when we leave most of them in the safe. And the more words we know, the surer and freer we are to choose the plainest, simplest words. After all, having knowledge is useful only if we can convey it clearly and briefly—and that means translating the complex into the simple. That can't happen when we write, as Virginia Woolf said, "as if thought plunged into a sea of words and came up dripping." (p. 38)

The antidote for obfuscation is simple: Write like you talk. When you write, instead of worrying about the "correct" way to frame a sentence, just put down the ideas as they come to you. When you finish, read it out loud. If you stumble over clauses and end each sentence out of breath, your sentences are too long. Try making them shorter.

When writers make something more complicated than it needs to be, they force readers to "translate" into understandable language. Too many readers just give up.

During the past 40 days, you have read about the qualities of good writing. Complexity wasn't one of them. As writing coach Donald Murray is fond of saying, "Less is more."

In Your Writer's Notebook . . .

Find and rewrite a piece of writing that's flabby or overwritten—it could be that you need to look no further than a memo from your central office. Failing that, you might use a computer instruction manual or something from a legal contract (the sale contract you signed when you bought your last car will work perfectly). If you still have a college textbook lying around, you can also find lots of overwritten prose and jargon. Just rewrite it so that it makes sense. You can also find examples of flabby prose by going into an Internet search engine (Google is good for this) and typing in the phrase "examples of bad writing" (be sure to put it in quotes). You'll get lots of hits.

In Your Classroom Writer's Workshop . . .

See appendix C, which compares the way bureaucrats write with the way advertising copywriters write. Let your students have a go at "translating" some of their jargon into everyday English.

You might also like to try rewriting some well-written prose (like the Gettysburg Address) into convoluted language, and letting students rewrite into clear language. Here's an example—first, Ecclesiastes 9:11 from the Old Testament, and then a wordy rewriting. Giving students the wordy version, letting them paraphrase into better writing, and then showing them the original, can help them see the value of clearly written prose.

> **The original:** I returned and saw under the sun, that the race is not to the swift, nor the battle to the strong, neither yet bread to the wise, nor yet riches to men of understanding, nor yet favor to men of skill; but time and chance happeneth to them all.

> **The "bad writing" version:** Objective consideration of contemporary phenomena compels the conclusion that success or failure in competitive activities exhibits no tendency to be commensurate with innate capacity, but that a considerable element of the unpredictable must invariably be taken into account.

"And We Will Teach Them How": The Craft of Teaching the Craft of Writing

> Education is not filling a pail but the lighting of a fire.
>
> *William Butler Yeats*

> The mediocre teacher tells. The good teacher explains. The superior teacher demonstrates. The great teacher inspires.
>
> *William Arthur Ward*

Writing is a complex activity and initiating novices into the practice in large classroom groups is no easy task. But the good news is that teaching writing—like the act of writing itself—is a craft. It can be learned. The premise of this book is that before we can teach writing effectively, we must experience writing for ourselves. It is a premise that goes without saying for teachers of every other skill. We just assume that Spanish conversation instructors should be Spanish speakers, that people who teach gourmet cooking should be gourmet cooks, that dancing teachers should themselves be comfortable—even proficient—on the dance floor.

And the first step toward mastering the craft of writing teaching is becoming a writing craftsperson yourself. But there are other qualities you'll need if you are to teach writing effectively. You'll need to care about students. Not just their writing abilities and their potential for academic achievement, but students as people. It's an educational cliché, but nonetheless true: Students don't care what we know until they know that we care. In writing conferencing, the first thing we do—before we try to help the writing get better—is to listen to the writer and react to what he or she has said. Many students have grown up to think that the reason they write is so that a teacher can look at it, correct it, assess it, and give them suggestions for improvement. How sad. They have never had a teacher who looked at their stories and reacted like a reader, not a grader. If a student writes about the death of his dog, he doesn't need to talk about leads or organization. He needs to talk about dogs and loss and feelings and the possibility of a new puppy. That helps him become invested in his piece and see how readers react. At that point, he's ready to learn about leads and organization.

The next step is to demonstrate the process by modeling writing. Modeling should involve three different activities: First, occasionally bring something to class that you have written. Bring your writer's notebook so they can see that you are a writer, too, and that you write outside of school. Nothing is more effective than saying to your class, "Last night I was writing about something that happened to me when I was roughly your age. I just wanted to read it to you today and see what you thought." Second, modeling means that students see you write in class. During the first few minutes of writing workshop, you yourself should write. Let students see you doing the same thing they are. Frequently they will ask you to share what you have written. Don't be afraid to read what you wrote, even if you don't think it's very good. And finally, modeling means that we occasionally "write out loud." That is, we demonstrate process by writing on a chart tablet or an overhead transparency, processing our thoughts and our writing decisions verbally as we go. That lets students see how writing actually works in the mind of a writer.

The final piece of the puzzle is to teach writing, craft element by craft element. The kind of writing teaching most of us remember was teachers who marked conventions and wrote general comments, good or bad, like "Good job!" or "Tell me more" or "Awkward" or "Rewrite this section." Perhaps we made a *C* and wanted to improve our piece, but we weren't told exactly how. We needed instruction in how to write a more effective lead or how to organize our piece better or how to use dialogue to add reader interest or how to describe a character or a place in a way that put pictures in the mind of a reader. Short, focused craft lessons (some teachers call them mini-lessons) give young writers the tools they need to improve their writing.

So we show students we care, we model the process, and we teach the craft elements of writing. In short, we share our enthusiasm for the craft and the techniques that bring it to life.

The result? The poet William Wordsworth (1888) probably expressed it best:

> *What we have loved,*
>
> *Others will love, and we will teach them how. . . .*

In Your Writer's Notebook . . .

Complete this statement in your writer's notebook: I would be a better writing teacher if . . . Reflect over what you have learned in the 40 writeaerobic workouts and set some goals for your teaching in the future. Perhaps you will want to list what you do well as a writing teacher and the ways you will seek improvement.

In Your Classroom Writer's Workshop . . .

Ask your students what is most effective for them in your writing classroom. Ask what strategies they enjoy most and which are the most effective in helping them become better writers. Let them complete this statement: I'd be a better writer if . . .

Appendix A

Literary Composting: Why Keep a Writer's Notebook?

> A writer's journal isn't like anyone else's. Other people can settle for outpourings to Dear Diary. Not writers. Our journals are where we exercise our imagination and craft, as a dancer works at the bar each day or a musician practices. There, we become our own best teachers.
>
> *Arno Karlen*

Carpenters experiment with woodworking in their workshops. Mechanics work on—and play with—engines in their garages. Sculptors work on new ideas in their studios. When a chef wants to try out new flavor combinations, he or she goes to a kitchen.

Writers don't need to add an extra room or convert unused space. All they need is a writer's notebook. For the writer, the notebook serves the same purpose as the workshop, the garage, the studio, and the kitchen. It's a place to experiment with writing.

Frequently people confuse writer's notebooks with journals or diaries. There are similarities, but they are not the same. A diary is a place to record the events of your life. A journal is a place to record not only what happened, but also what you thought about it. If you watch a sunset at the beach, you might write about what you did in your diary. But if you end up writing for several days about how sunsets make you feel, you are probably keeping a journal, not a diary.

Writers frequently put the events of their lives in their writer's notebooks, so they do often read like diaries. And they sometimes react to those events, so they can resemble journals. But writers don't stop there. Let's say you're working on your ability to paint word pictures with description—you may well spend several days describing the ocean sunset, not so much because it was personally important or moving for you as because you just want to develop your ability to write description. There are many reasons to keep a dairy or a journal, but only one reason to write regularly in a writer's notebook: to improve your writing.

Sometimes woodworkers go into their shop and just start tinkering with a piece of wood. They just returned from a craft store and saw a duck carved from wood, and now they just want to know if they can do one, too. And sometimes, in mid-duck, they decide the carving should be a swan instead. They're just playing with wood, partly to see what happens when they try something new and partly to further develop their ability to carve.

Writers do that, too. True, some days their writer's notebook will record events and thoughts, like diaries and journals. But writers are always looking for opportunities to improve their skills and to try something new. *Writeaerobics* will help you develop a writer's notebook. The entries are varied enough for you to see the possibilities in keeping a notebook, and when you finish you'll be a better writing teacher—and you'll also have a start toward a lifetime habit of keeping a writer's notebook. Plus, you'll see how you can use the writer's notebook concept with your students.

To help you think more concretely about what you might find in a typical writer's notebook kept by a teacher (a writer/teacher would obviously include more entries that deal with writing pedagogy), here's a listing of what you might find. The numbers following the types of entries indicate the *Writeaerobics* workout that will help you with that type of writer's notebook entry. Writer's notebooks may include:

- Reactions to literature (2, 10, 19)
- Writing about your own writing process (5, 7, 25, 30, 36)
- Reflecting on your own history as a writer (5, 15)
- Just compiling a list of future writing topics so you always have something to write about (8)
- Analyzing literary devices (18)
- Listing words and phrases you like from the work of other authors (38)
- Copying leads or endings you like from the work of other authors (28)
- Analyzing the grammar of a piece you wrote or a paragraph you copied from another author (21, 33)
- Not writing at all, but going back to rewrite something you wrote earlier (23, 24, 26, 39)
- Copying sentences that contain great verbs from other authors (29)
- Making a list from your own reading of various types of story problems/conflicts/obstacles faced by characters (32)
- Self-imposed writing exercises that you got from books on writing (37)
- Making a list from your own reading of words and phrases you like (39)
- Freewriting (3)
- Writing descriptions that show, not tell (12, 13)
- Practicing literary devices, like dialogue (22) or flashbacks (31)
- Telling stories on paper as a way to practice the storytelling craft (14)
- Not writing at all, but instead interacting with a well written piece of prose or poetry by reading out loud (11)

Writer's notebooks are a type of literary compost. They offer writers the opportunity to collect words and phrases and ideas that they might want to include in their writing, to play with literary devices, and to reflect on their own writing and writing-teaching. In school, we learn to work on complete projects and to finish what we start. But that's bad advice for the writer's notebook. If you want to work on improving description, you might just describe things and people—out of context of any story or theme. Or just write dialogue that doesn't fit into any piece you're working on. Or maybe just write leads that you never develop into a finished piece.

The writer's notebook is a place for writers to play and work and experiment. Sometimes those experiments can be developed into pieces you'll be proud of.

Playing With Leads:
The Escaped Python Story

Here's a craft lesson on lead writing you can do with your students. Below is a story, told chronologically, about a boy whose pet python escaped. It's a simple story with a beginning, a middle, and an end. The story is provided so everyone will be working "on the same page" when it comes to lead writing—everyone in your writing workshop will have the same story facts.

Let students experiment with leads from the facts given. Then you can share various types of leads that could have been written from the same facts. Examples of those leads from other books and stories are also provided.

Make a chart of the lead types and leave it up in your classroom; you'll find that students will refer to it frequently during writing workshop. The section of this appendix under the heading "Looking at Leads Like a Writer" gives you additional information to use in building craft lessons on lead-writing.

The Escaped Python Story

There was a boy named Billy and he lived in Yourtown with his parents.

Sometimes, when his mom and dad went out at night, they left him with a babysitter.

The baby sitter's name was Rachel. She was a teen-ager, a senior in high school.

Billy was in the fourth grade.

He had a dog, but he had always wanted a snake.

Billy made all *A*'s and *B*'s the second six weeks, so his dad bought him a snake.

It was a python.

Billy loved his python and named him Henry.

One night when Billy went to feed Henry, he was surprised.

Henry wasn't in his habitat in Billy's room

He looked under the bed and in the closet—he looked everywhere in his room.

As he was looking behind his dresser, he heard a scream from downstairs.

It was Rachel, who was babysitting him that night.

"Eeeeeeek! It's a snake. There's a snake loose here! It's huge! I'm calling 911."

As Billy ran downstairs, he heard glass breaking.

Rachel had crashed through a picture window to escape from Henry.

A police car drove up with its lights flashing and its sirens on.

Paramedics ran up the driveway to help Rachel.

She was still sobbing and her face was covered in blood from the cuts the glass made.

Henry crawled up on the couch next to the broken-out window and calmly watched the commotion outside.

Lead Types and References

Begin With Dialogue

"Eeeeeeek! It's a snake. There's a snake loose here."

Billy heard his baby sitter's screams downstairs as he looked under his bed for his pet python Henry.

"I'm tired of remembering," Hannah said to her mother as she climbed into the car. She was flushed with April sun and her mouth felt sticky from jelly beans and Easter candy.

The Devil's Arithmetic

"I'll race you to the corner, Ellen!" Annemarie adjusted the thick leather pack on her back so that her schoolbooks balanced evenly. "Ready?" she looked at her best friend.

Number the Stars

Begin With Internal Monologue

There's no way, Billy thought, that his snake could have escaped from his room. He just had to be in there somewhere.

Just then, the screaming started downstairs.

Before Buck, before I knew the word stepfather, I thought of the pieces of my life as normal and normal-sized.

Framed in Fire

Begin With a Question

Why would a normal fourth grader want a python for a pet?

You ever see ink mixed up with blood? That's what's getting set down on this paper. It's my blood, too. No one else's.

The Journal of Augustus Pelletier: The Lewis and Clark Expedition

Begin With a Character Introducing Himself/Herself

I may as well tell you now and get it over with. I'm the fourth grader whose python got loose and caused his babysitter to crash through a plate glass window.

My name is India Opal Buloni, and last summer my daddy, the preacher, sent me to the store for a box of macaroni-and-cheese, some white rice, and two tomatoes and I came back with a dog. This is what happened: I walked into the produce section of the Winn-Dixie grocery store to pick out my two tomatoes and I almost bumped right into the store manager. He was standing there all red-faced, screaming and waving his arms around.

Because of Winn-Dixie

Begin With Narrator Introducing a Character

Rachel was not an adventurous teen-ager, or especially brave. That's why she thought babysitting was a good way to make money. After all, what could possibly happen while you spent several hours watching a nice kid like Billy?

They say Maniac Magee was born in a dump. They say his stomach was a cereal box and his heart a sofa spring.

They say he kept an eight-inch cockroach on a leash and that rats stood guard over him while he slept.

Manic Magee

Henry Huggins' dog Ribsy was a plain ordinary city dog, the kind of dog that strangers usually called Mutt or Pooch. They always called him this in a friendly way, because Ribsy was a friendly dog.

Ribsy

Begin With a Character Summarizing the Story

I suppose I should have been more careful with my snake. I just never realized he could cause such trouble if he got loose. He did get loose, and it turned out to be the biggest event that's ever happened on my street.

I suppose I can't really blame my parents for not believing me when I told them about the weirdness under my bed. After all, adults never believe a kid when he or she talks about that kind of thing. Oh, they'll believe you're afraid, of course. But they never believe you've actually got a good reason to feel that way.

"There's Nothing Under My Bed" in
Bruce Coville's Book of Nightmares

Begin With Background Information

Most people are afraid of snakes. But as long as Billy could remember, he had loved them. That's why he asked for a python when his father offered to reward him for good grades.

There was no lake at Camp Green Lake. There once was a very large lake there, the largest lake in Texas. That was over a hundred years ago. Now it is just a dry, flat wasteland.

Holes

Begin With Description

A police cruiser pulled into Billy's driveway with its lights flashing and its siren blaring. Paramedics in white uniforms sprinted up the driveway to help the babysitter, still screaming with her face covered in blood after she crashed through a plate glass window.

Stretched out on top of the couch, surveying the whole scene, Billy's pet python Henry watched the front-yard drama unfolding.

The tropical rain fell in drenching sheets, hammering the corrugated roof of the clinic building, roaring down the metal gutters, splashing on the ground in a torrent.

Jurassic Park

We were afraid to go too close to the house. So we stayed down at the street, staring up at it. Staring across the bare, sloping front yard.

No grass would grow in that yard. The trees, gnarled and bent, were all dead. Not even weeds sprouted in the dry, cracked dirt.

At the top of the sloping yard, the house seemed to stare back at us.

"The House of No Return" in *Tales to Give You Goosebumps*

A soft rain slips down through the trees and the smell of ocean is so strong that it can almost be licked off the air. Trucks rumble along Rogers Street and men in t-shirts stained with fishblood shout to each other from the decks of boats. Beneath them the ocean swells up against the black pilings and sucks back down to the barnacles. Beer cans and old pieces of Styrofoam rise and fall and pools of spilled diesel fuel undulate like huge iridescent jellyfish.

The Perfect Storm

Begin Near the Problem

Note: For these leads, the characters typically are not introduced first. It's like you started reading in the middle of the story. You have names thrown at you with no indication of when this happened or where it happened or how old the characters are or why they have a problem. All that comes later. The author is just trying to get you hooked on the story from the very first.

The python habitat was empty. It took a minute for it to sink in. Somewhere in Billy's house, a 10-foot python was loose, and Billy didn't know where it was.

Bertie Kidd was bored.

The Bathwater Gang

It was almost December, and Jonas was beginning to be frightened.

The Giver

One day Grandfather wouldn't get out of bed. He just lay there and stared at the ceiling and looked sad.

At first little Willy thought he was playing.

Stone Fox

Looking at Leads Like a Writer

One of the best ways to become a good lead writer is to study the leads of other writers. The best time to analyze a lead is after you've read the entire piece. Then you can better see just what the writer has done in the lead.

What should you look for?

- First, what type of lead was it?

  Dialogue

  Interior monologue

  Question

  Character introduces himself/herself

  Narrator introduces main character

  A character summarizes story

  Background information on the story

  Description

  Beginning near the problem

  Or some other category that doesn't fit those above?

  (Note: Some leads will be combinations of two or more of these categories.)

- Is it told first-person or third-person? Who is telling the story?

- Analyze the grammar. Identify subjects, verbs, adjectives, adverbs.

- Try rewriting the lead into another type. If it's a dialogue lead, try making it an interior monologue lead. If it's a background lead, try re-casting it to begin near the story's problem (after you've read far enough to identify the problem).

- Try to think of the reason the author used the lead. For example, there is a difference between stories and narratives. Stories have a problem or conflict. Narratives are a chronological recounting of events. Narratives may contain minor problems, but they are not the focus of the piece. *The Giver* (Lowry, 1993) is a story and *Because of Winn-Dixie* (DiCamillo, 2000) is a narrative. Note how stories frequently begin with the problem/conflict, and narratives (which don't have a conflict) will begin by introducing the character.

References for Appendix B

Cleary, B. 1964. *Ribsy*. New York: Dell.

Coville, B. 1995. There's nothing under the bed. In *Bruce Coville's book of nightmares* (pp. 1–37). New York: Scholastic.

Crichton, M. 1990. *Jurassic park*. New York: Ballantine.

DiCamillo, K. 2000. *Because of Winn-Dixie*. Cambridge, Mass.: Candlewick Press.

Gardiner, J. R. 1980. *Stone fox*. New York: Harper Trophy.

Junger, S. 1997. *The perfect storm*. New York: Harper Paperbacks.

Lasky, K. 2000. *The journal of Augustus Pelletier: The Lewis and Clark expedition.* New York: Scholastic.

Lowry, L. 1989. *Number the stars.* New York: Dell.

Lowry, L. 1993. *The giver.* Boston: Houghton Mifflin.

Patneaude, D. 1999. *Framed in fire.* Morton Grove, Ill.: Albert Whitman.

Spinelli, J. 1990. *Maniac Magee.* Boston: Little, Brown.

Spinelli, J. 1990. *The bathwater gang.* Boston: Little, Brown.

Stine, R. L. 1994. The house of no return. In *Tales to give you goosebumps* (pp. 1–14). New York: Scholastic.

Yolen, J. 1990. *The devil's arithmetic.* New York: Viking Penguin.

Appendix C

Learning From Advertising Copywriters: Writing Simply

If you have intermediate-level students or older, they'll enjoy playing with these ads that sound like they were written by college professors or bureaucrats. It's a good way to illustrate that big words and long sentences typically don't make for good writing. The overwritten version comes first, followed by the ad slogan as it actually appeared. Your young writers will enjoy decoding the gobbledygook. You might let them try it the other way around, too: Give them an ad slogan and let them try to rewrite it using long sentences and words they mined from a thesaurus.

It is advisable to effect an expeditious execution of your present project on the earliest timetable, with the purpose of facilitating achievement of the goals implicit in your attentions.

The original: Nike: Just do it.

The purpose of this communication is to ascertain whether you are sufficiently provisioned with the lactic secretions of bovines.

The original: Got milk?

The beverage is represented as functioning in a manner that generally facilitates the interactivity of interpersonal processes.

The original: Things go better with Coke.

Comparable to hardness and durability characteristics associated with certain geological categories, but specifically not with friable sedimentary types of aerated igneous pumices.

The original: Chevy: Like a rock.

Cogitate in a manner that is immediately distinguishable from the processes of thinking employed by others.

The original: Apple: Think different.

Appendix D

Books on Writing and Illustrating: Helping Young Authors Identify With Their Older Counterparts

The power of writing workshop is that young writers are using the same creative processes used by professional writers. Good writing teachers constantly show that all writing is much the same. Everyone has to conceive an idea, wrestle with it, play with the language in multiple drafts, then revise and edit it. Some ideas result in books that are published. Some don't.

So good writing teachers look for opportunities to share as much as they can about the lives and work habits of professional writers—especially writers their class enjoys. The books below are just a sampling of the many books available on how professional writers and illustrators move an idea from conception to publication.

Aliki. (1986). *How a book is made*. New York: Harper Trophy.

Christelow, E. (1995). *What do authors do?* New York: Clarion.

Christelow, E. (1999). *What do illustrators do?* New York: Clarion.

Nixon, J. (1988). *If you were a writer*. New York: Aladdin Paperbacks.

Stevens, J. (1995). *From pictures to words: A book about making a book*. New York: Holiday House.

You can find lots of information on individual writers on the Internet. Go to any good search engine (like *Dogpile* or *Google*, for instance) and type in the name of the writer in quotations. (If you don't put quotes around the name, the search engine looks for instances of the first name and the second name, but not necessarily together. So a search for Eric Carle (without quotes around his name) would yield, for instance, information about Eric the Red and ERIC, the educational database.

And if you teach middle school or older writers, be sure your classroom library includes some books written for older writers. You'll find these in the writer's section of any good bookstore, or search online for Writer's Digest Press, which publishes many books for professional writers. In addition to books already cited in the References of this book, like *Word Painting* (McClanahan, 1999) and *Writing Dialogue* (Chiarella, 1998), you'll find many practical books on writing mysteries, writing poetry, crafting effective leads, and the like. Don't worry that they are written for adult writers; you'll probably find that they are easier to read and more user-friendly than most language arts textbooks.

References

Abercrombie, B. (1990). *Charlie Anderson*. New York: McElderry.

Babbit, N. (1975). *Tuck everlasting*. New York: Farrar, Straus, Giroux.

Bierce, A. (1970). An Occurrence at Owl Creek Bridge. In J. Hopkins (Ed.), *The complete short stories of Ambrose Bierce* (pp. ??) Lincoln, NE: University of Nebraska Press.

Cambourne, B. (1988). *The whole story: Natural learning the acquisition of literacy in the classroom*. Auckland, New Zealand: Ashton Scholastic.

Cameron, J. (1998). *The right to write: An invitation and initiation into the writing life*. New York: Tarcher/Putnam.

Chiarella, T. (1998). *Writing dialogue*. Cincinnati, OH: Story Press.

Cisneros, S. (1984). *The house on Mango Street*. New York: Vintage.

Clark, R. (Winter 2002). The songs of writers. *Poynter Workbench*, *7*, 10.

Dickens, C. (1859). *A tale of two cities*. New York: Heritage Press.

Frank, M. (1995). *If you're trying to teach kids how to write . . . you gotta have this book!* Nashville, TN: Incentive Publications.

Higgins, G. (1990). *On writing*. New York: Henry Holt.

Hillocks, G. (2002). *The testing trap*. New York: Teachers College Press.

Houston, G. (1992). *But no candy*. New York: Philomel.

Houston, G. (1994). *Mountain Valor*. New York: Philomel.

LaRocque, P. (December 20, 2002). Use large words sparingly. *Quill*, *90*, (9), 38.

Lesser, C. (1997). *Storm on the desert*. San Diego: Harcourt Brace.

MacLachlan, P. (1985). *Sarah, plain and tall*. New York: Scholastic.

Martin, B. Jr., & Archambault, J. (1985). *The ghost-eye tree*. New York: Henry Holt.

Martin, B. Jr. & Archambault, J. (1986). *White Dynamite and Curly Kidd*. New York: Holt, Rinehart, and Winston.

Martin, B. Jr., & Archambault, J. (1988). *Listen to the rain*. New York: Henry Holt.

Martin, B. Jr., & Kellogg, S. (1998). *A beasty story*. San Diego: Harcourt.

McClanahan, R.(1999). *Word painting: A guide to writing more descriptively.* Cincinnati, OH: Writer's Digest Books.

McLuhan, M. (1962). *The Gutenberg galaxy: The making of typographic man.* Toronto: University of Toronto Press.

Murray, D. (1987). *Write to learn.* New York: Holt, Rinehart and Winston.

O'Connor, P. (1999). *Words fail me: What everyone who writes should know about writing.* Orlando, FL: Harcourt.

Peck, R. N. (1980). *The secrets of successful fiction.* Cincinnati, OH: Writer's Digest Books.

Rowling, J. K. (1999*). Harry Potter and the chamber of secrets.* New York: Scholastic.

Rule, R., & Wheeler, S. (1993). *Creating the story: Guides for writers.* Portsmouth, NH: Heinemann.

Saltzman, J. (1993). *If you can talk, you can write.* New York: Warner Books.

Scieszka, J. (1991). *Knights of the kitchen table.* New York: Penguin Puffin.

Scieszka, J. (1989). *The true story of the 3 little pigs!* New York: Viking Penguin.

Spandel, V., & Stiggins, R. (1997). *Creating writers: Linking writing assessment and instruction.* New York: Longman.

Spandel, V. (2001). *Creating writers: Linking writing assessment and instruction (3rd ed).* New York: Longman.

Spandel, V. (2002). *Write traits teacher's guide, grade 4.* Wilmington, MA: Great Source.

Thomason, T., & York, C. (2002). *Absolutely write! Teaching the craft elements of writing.* Norwood, MA: Christopher-Gordon.

Wells, R. (1996). *Divine secrets of the Ya-Ya Sisterhood.* New York: HarperCollins.

White, E. B. (1952). *Charlotte's web.* New York: Harper & Row.

Whitlock, B. (1986). *Educational myths I have known and loved.* New York: Shocken Books.

Wilhelm, J. (March 2001). Undoing the great grammatical scam! *Voices From the Middle, 8,* (3), 62.

Wordsworth, W. (1888). The Prelude. In *The complete poetical works.* London: Macmillan and Co.

Index

About the Author

Tommy Thomason is a former professional journalist who is now chairman of the Department of Journalism at Texas Christian University in Fort Worth. He also brings the perspective of a professional writer into elementary school and secondary classrooms, where he conducts writing workshops with young writers every week. Dr. Thomason is the author of *More Than a Writing Teacher: How to Become a Teacher Who Writes* and *Writer to Writer: How to Conference Young Authors.* He is co-author of *Write on Target: Preparing Young Writers to Succeed on State Writing Achievement Tests* and *Absolutely Write! Teaching the Craft Elements of Writing.*